Ida Stiefel

St. Pauls Bazaar Kochbuch

Ida Stiefel

St. Pauls Bazaar Kochbuch

ISBN/EAN: 9783742896230

Hergestellt in Europa, USA, Kanada, Australien, Japan

Cover: Foto ©Lupo / pixelio.de

Manufactured and distributed by brebook publishing software
(www.brebook.com)

Ida Stiefel

St. Pauls Bazaar Kochbuch

St. Pauls

azaar Kochbuch,

und

Geschaeftsfuehrer.

Herausgegeben von

IDA STIEFEL und MINNIE JACOBS.

Chicago,

1892.

Druck von Fred Kressmann & Bro., 140-146 Monroe St.

ESTABLISHED 1866.

William Schick,
Furniture & Carpet Emporium.

Indem wir hiermit unser

⚛︎Bazaar Kochbuch⚛︎

seiner Bestimmung übergeben, drängt es uns, zu-
vörderst unseren herzlichen Dank allen Freunden
auszusprechen, die in so überaus liebenswürdiger
Weise uns in der Herausgabe desselben behülflich
gewesen sind. Ferner sprechen wir die zuversicht-
liche Hoffnung aus, daß die lieben Leserinnen in
unserem kleinen Buche Etwas finden werden, das ihnen
die oft so beschwerliche Arbeit in Küche und Speise-
zimmer erleichtern kann. Wir glauben, daß der kleine Band werthvolle
Dienste leisten wird, da die Recepte und Anweisungen nicht etwa aus der
Erfahrung e i n e r tüchtigen Hausfrau und Köchin stammen, sondern von
einer g r o ß e n A n z a h l erfahrener Damen uns geliefert worden sind.
Diese Lieblings-Recepte unserer vielen Mitarbeiterinnen sind erprobt
worden und tragen die Empfehlung ihrer Verfasserinnen mit sich. Die
allermeisten sind Original-Recepte, die in k e i n e m a n d e r e n Buche
zu finden sind. Da die Einsenderinnen aus allen Theilen Amerika's und
Deutschland's stammen, so erhalten wir durch ihre Beiträge die Lieblings-
Speisen der verschiedensten Gegenden.

Möge dieses Buch nicht nur ein kleines Andenken an die Bazaar-
Feier (1892) des Frauen Vereins und Jugend Vereins unserer lieben
St. Pauls Kirche — La Salle Ave. und Ohio Str. — bilden, sondern
sich auch ein bescheidenes Plätzchen erobern im Schränkchen der Hausfrau, in dem sie die Bücher verwahrt, die sie liebt, weil sie nützlich
sind. — — — Den Schlüssel zu solchem Schränkchen aber lasse man
hübsch stecken, damit auch die „Herren der Schöpfung" sich manchmal aus
dem G e s c h ä f t s f ü h r e r des Buches einen Rath holen können.

Die Verfasserinnen.

Zither Instructions.

A few more pupils will be accepted by

Ad. Maurer,

31 E. PEARSON ST.

WM. RUSCHE,

WHOLESALE AND RETAIL DEALER IN

ELGIN DAIRY MILK,

Hotels, Restaurants and Families supplied.

No. 18
GERMANIA PLACE.

LOUIS HAAKE,

Staple & Fancy Groceries,

74 WELLS STREET.

Suppen.

Spargel Suppe. — Frischer Spargel, in kleine Stücke geschnitten, wird gar gekocht. Das Wasser wird durch ein Sieb gegossen und der Spargel beiseite gesetzt. In einen Topf kommt ½ Pfd. Butter, ¼ Pfd. Mehl und dann das Spargel-Wasser. Nach einer ¼ Stunde wird der Spargel dazu gethan. Man giebt das nöthige Salz dazu und rührt die Suppe mit 2 Eidottern an.

Frau M. Panneberg.

Suppe mit Fleischklößen. — ½ Pfd. fein gehacktes Rindfleisch, 3 Eßlöffel Butter fein gerührt, 2 Eidotter, 2 Semmeln eingeweicht und ausgedrückt, Muskatnuß, Salz und zuletzt der Schaum von einem Eiweiß. Die Masse muß zwar weich sein, aber doch zusammen halten. Man kocht 10 Minuten in der Fleisch-Suppe.

M. W.

Apfelwein-Suppe. — 1½ Qt. Apfelwein, ½ Qt. Wasser, einige Stückchen Zimmt und Zucker nach Geschmack wird zugedeckt zum Kochen gebracht. Unterdeß zerrührt man 1 Kochlöffel Mehl und ½ Qt. Wasser fein, läßt es gut durchkochen, stellt es vom Feuer, giebt 1 Qt. kochende Milch dazu und rührt die Suppe mit 2 Eidottern an.

W. Sch.

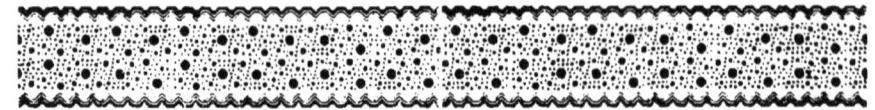

Charles L. Meyers,

 # GROCERIES,

Best Brands of Flour.

PROVISIONS, TEAS, COFFEES,

SPICES & FRUITS,

471 N. CLARK STREET,

Orders called for and delivered.

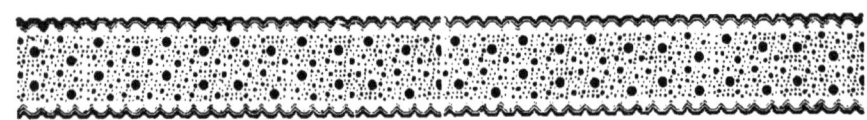

Kraut = Suppe. — Für 6 Personen: ½ Pfd. Spinat, Hand=
voll Körbelkraut, 2 Stengel Krausemünze, Schnittzwiebeln und etwas
Majoran. Hacke zusammen recht fein und presse den Saft aus, daß
Kraut trocken sei. Dann laß einen Löffel voll Butter heiß werden,
dämpfe das Kraut darin bis es weich ist, doch nicht zu lange, sonst zieht
es Wasser. Dann rühre eine Handvoll Mehl darein, gieße Fleischbrühe
dazu so viel als man Suppe haben will, Salz und ein wenig fein ge=
schnittenes Brod. Laß dies zusammen eine ¼ Stunde kochen, richte an
und rühre ein wohl geschlagenes Eigelb, etwas Rahm und Muskatnuß
darein.

Frau E. Buerki

VIRGINIA MOCK-TURTLE-SOUP. — 1 large calf's head well
cleaned and washed, ½ can corn, ½ can butterbeans, 1 can tomatoes, 3 large potatoes cut in small pieces, ½ lemon cut in thin
slices, 1 wine glass of sherry, 2 table spoons of Worcestershire
sauce, cloves, whole pepper, brown flour, brown butter. Lay het
head in salt water 24 hours, changing the water several times.
After the head has been well cleaned and the brain removed put
on to boil in salt water enough to cover. Let boil until the meat
drops from the bone. When cool cut all the meat, including the
tongue, into small bits. Strain the stock while hot. Then put
on the meat, corn, potatoes, butter beans, tomatoes, with stock
enough to cover, when tender add brains, cloves and pepper, stir 2
tablespoons of browned flour rubbed smooth in 1 tablespoon of
melted butter, let it boil up well and finish the seasoning
by the addition of wine, Worcestershire and slices of lemon.

Mrs. EMILIE W. JOHN.

AGNES WENZEL'S FAVORITE VEGETABLE SOUP. — ½ doz.
corn, 1 qt. butterbeans, 1 qt. tomatoes, 3 large potatoes, 5 cent
soup bone, 4 qts. water. Boil the bone and water down to 2 qts.
then strain put on all the vegetables with the stock and boil until
all are tender.

Mrs EMILIE W. JOHN.

—10—

TOMATO SOUP. — Take a good piece of beef and make stock. In this put a carrot cut in fine pieces, a little rice, a piece of celery root, a small piece of bacon, a little pepper and salt to taste, a small onion, a little Worcestershire sauce and then add a can of tomatoes which have been boiled and strained.

Mrs. J. TIEDEMANN.

——

BEAN SOUP. — Soak 1 qt of beans over night, then boil in 3 qts. of water. For flavoring use a bit of carrot and a little onion, with either shavings of celery or celery salt. Strain through a colander when it is done. Then pour into it 1 cup of hot cream or milk. Serve with little squares of toasted bread.

IDA SCHMIDT.

——

TOMATO SOUP. — Boil together for 2 hours, 3 lbs. of beef in 4 qts. of water, 1 can of tomatoes, 1 turnip, 1 bunch of soup greens, 1 small head of cabbage and 4 carrots. Stir separately 2 well beaten eggs, $\frac{1}{4}$ cup of water or milk, adding enough flour to thicken, drop into the soup, let it come to a boil and serve.

Mrs. FRED MILLINGTON.

——

SWISS RECIPE FOR INVALIDS. — Brown small slices of bread in a pan, add tablespoonful of butter and stir. Add 1 teaspoonful of flour and brown, pour boiling water to it, half full, then beat 1 egg, pour in and stir. Grate nutmeg, add pinch of salt and let it come to a boil.

ELIZA TANNER.

Suppe von jungen Erbsen. — Die Erbsen läßt man, ohne sie zu waschen, in einem Stück zergangener Butter eine Weile schwitzen, sowie auch später je nach der Portion der Suppe, 1–2 Löffel Mehl darin anziehen, doch muß letzteres weiß bleiben. Dann gießt man die nöthige Quantität Bouillon oder kochendes Wasser und etwas Fleisch Extract hinein und wenn die Erbsen gar sind, Salz und gehackte Petersilie. Man koche Fleisch oder Grießklöße darin oder gebe in Butter geröstetes Weißbrot dazu. Zeit des Kochens 1 Stunde.

Katharina Timm.

———

CREAM OF TOMATO SOUP. — Take six good-sized tomatoes. a small onion and piece of celery. pepper and salt to taste. Boil till done, then strain and add one Quart of beef broth. Let it boil up and stir in slowly one cup of hot cream.

Mrs. M. EMMERICH.

———

Fleisch.

———

Ragout von gebratenem Kalbfleisch. — Drei Eßlöffel voll braunes Mehl in Butter, Wasser, Lorbeerblätter, Zwiebel, Citronen und Nelkenpfeffer. Dann das Fleisch dazu. Gut durchkochen.

Helene Lüpsch.

———

Zungen-Koteletten mit Spinat. Eine weichgetochte frische Ochsenzunge wird abgezogen, in fingerdicke Scheiben geschnitten, in geschlagenes Ei getaucht, mit geriebener Semmel überstreut u. dann in Butter gebraten, worauf man sie als Beilage zu Spinat giebt.

Marie Pfeifner.

—14—

BEEF A LA MODE. — Put a nice piece of beef in a dish with salt, pepper, onion, cloves, allspice, juniper berries, bayleaves, vinegar and a little bacon. Let stand for 3 days, then boil 4 hours.

CLARA DETMER.

BEEF A LA MODE. Use short rib pieces or part of rump. Take out all bones, have well rolled up and put in a piece of new muslin to keep it in place, add a piece of butter and rub well with pepper and salt. Brown slowly in frying pan with a few slices of baked onions, carrot, celery, and a bit of butter. Remove to a soupkettle, add cloves, bayleaf, lemon, cook 1½ hours, add a small cup of vinegar. When meat is tender take out and make a cream sauce of both stews and serve with roast potatoes.

Mrs. HARMONING.

—

VEAL LOAF. Three pounds of leg or loin of veal and ¾ pound of salt pork chopped fine; roll 12 crackers, put half of them in the veal with 2 eggs, season with pepper and salt, not much salt as the pork is salty; mix all together and make into a solid form, then take the crackers that are left and spread over the loaf, bake one hour, basting occasionally and slice cold.

Mrs. G. L. SCHIRMER.

—

JELLIED CHICKEN. — Cut up a chicken, cover with water, add knuckle of veal, spice with pepper, salt, onion, a very little nutmeg, a pinch of red pepper, 2 cloves, 1 bayleaf, and boil till tender. Take out the chicken, put in a dish, pour broth through a cloth, add ½ cup vinegar, pour over chicken, mix and let stand till next day.

Mrs. H. SCHROEDER.

Mrs. J. Schieferstein,

Schuhe u. Stiefel

303 E. Division St.

ESTABLISHED 1866.

C. M. WEINBERGER,

Druggist and Apothecary,

219 North Wells St.,

Corner Chicago Ave.

TELEPHONE NORTH-274.

FRED J. HOFFMAN,

Dealer in

Fine Teas and Groceries,

414 GARFIELD AVENUE,

near Larrabee Street.

M. SCHELL,

Bakery, Ice Cream, Stationery,

SCHOOL SUPPLIES, ETC.

230 N. State St.

Wir geben an verschiedenen Stellen
einige leere Blätter zu, die für das Abschreiben solcher
Recepte bestimmt sind, die man hier und da findet
und gerne aufbewahren möchte. Es kann
somit jede Köchin das Buch nach
Gutdünken bereichern.

SAVORY PYRAMID. — May be made of beef, veal, pork, mutton or lamb. Break 3 eggs into a basin and beat until light and frothy, then stir into them by degrees 6 tablespoonfuls of fine breadcrumbs, 2 ounces of butter slightly melted, a tablespoon of finely minced parsly, a tablespoon of finely minced powdered herbs, one teaspoon of seasoning, ¾ of a lb. of meat chopped fine, then put in gravy, mix thoroughly, form into pyramid shape, eggcoat with breadcrumbs, bake in greased tin, and serve with gravy poured around.

Mrs. OTTO SOMMER.

———

CHICKEN PIE. — Boil your chicken until tender and season, line deep dish with nice crust, put in the chicken, some sliced potatoes, and the gravy in which the chicken has boiled, add a teaspoonful of flour, cover with the crust, bake one hour.

•   Mrs. J. H. HAAKE.

———

MELTON VEAL. — Take any cold veal, either roasted or boiled, chop it fine and season with salt and pepper and lemon juice, add two or three tablespoonfuls of cracker crumbs and moisten with soup stock or hot water. Take ⅓ as much finely chopped ham as of veal, season with mustard and cayenne pepper, add one tablespoonful of cracker crumbs and moisten with stock or hot water. Butter a mould and line it with slices of hard boiled eggs. Put in the mixtures irregularly, so that it will have a mottled appearance when cut, press it closely and steam ¾ of an hour, set it away to cool, remove from mould and slice before serving.

CAROLINE NOEHREN.

———

—17

—18—

Sauerbraten. Man nimmt entweder Hammel oder Rindfleisch, legt es 4 Tage in Essig, Zwiebeln, weißen Pfeffer und Lorbeerblätter, dreht es Morgens und Abends von einer Seite zur andern, bratet es dann, belegt mit Speck und 1 Löffel Butter nebst etwas von dem Essig, in dem es lag, eine Stunde. Dann brennt man etwas Mehl, thut den übrigen Essig dazu mit einem Glas Wein, etwas Rum und einem kleinen Lebkuchen, läßt dies aufkochen, rührt es durch ein Sieb und schüttet es über den Braten. Eine Stunde langsam zu kochen.

Frau M. Panneberg.

Kartoffeln, Schweinsrippe und saure Aepfel zusammen gebraten. — Man setzt in einer etwas flachen Bratpfanne ein Stück Schweinsrippe zur Hälfte mit Wasser bedeckt und etwas Salz fest zugedeckt in einen nicht zu heißen Ofen und läßt 1 – 1¼ Stunde langsam kochen und gelblich braten. Alsdann nimmt man es heraus, belegt die Pfanne mit kleinen, rundgeschälten Kartoffeln, streut ein wenig Salz darüber, legt die Rippe darauf, und zwar die offene Seite nach oben, füllt die Höhlung derselben mit geschälten, in 4 Theile geschnittenen, sauren Aepfeln, gibt eine Tasse Wasser dazu, bedeckt die Pfanne und läßt die Kartoffeln darin langsam weich und gelb braten, während man sie einmal umdreht. Dann legt man die Rippe mit den Aepfeln in eine tiefe Schüssel und garniert sie mit den Kartoffeln.

Frau Ida Haack.

Gänsepfeffer. — Man putzt Kopf, Flügel, Füße, Hals, Magen, brüht Kopf und Füße ab und schält die harte Haut von Schnabel und Füßen und siedet sie weich in Salzwasser. Hernach röstet man Mehl in Butter, dämpft klein geschnittene Zwiebeln darin, löscht sie mit der Brühe vom Gänsepfeffer und dem Gänseblut, welches gleich beim Schlachten mit etwas Essig verrührt wurde, ab, thut Pfeffer und Nelken Citronenrädchen, Lorbeerblätter und den Gänsepfeffer hinein und läßt es bis zur gehörigen Dicke kochen.

Frau Schöller.

19

JOHN C. RICE,

STOVES,

Hardware,

House
Furnishing
Goods,

Manfacturers of

Tin, Copper and Sheet Iron Ware

494 WELLS ST.

Furnaces cleaned and repaired.

G. Gottmanshausen,

——DEALER IN——

Fresh and Salt Meats,

Vegetables, Poultry, Game, Fish, Dried Beef, Hams, Sausages, Etc.

500 NORTH CLARK STREET.

Families, Boarding Houses and Hotels supplied at reasonable rates.

Kalbsbraten.—Das Fleisch wird mit einem reinen Tuche gut abgeputzt und mit Salz gerieben. Dann läßt man in einer Pfanne Butter heiß werden, bringt das Fleisch nebst einigen Stückchen Brodkruste und Zwiebeln hinzu, läßt es langsam schön braun braten, füllt es mit Wasser auf, läßt es wieder ganz einkochen und nochmals auf beiden Seiten schön braun braten. Nun füllt man mit Fleischbrühe auf, läßt es recht langsam kochen bis der Braten weich genug ist und rührt sauren Rahm an die Sauce.

Clara Lathomus.

Falscher Rehbraten. — Man nehme eine Hammelkeule und lege sie 6-8 Tage in saure Milch, oder in süße mit einem Guße Essig. Man spickt oder bereitet ganz einfach wie Rehbraten. Am besten schmecken Teltower Rübchen oder irgend ein gewürziges Compot dazu.

Maria Conrad.

Deutscher Sauerbraten. — Man nehme ein schönes mageres Stück Rindfleisch von circa 6 Pfund, spickt es mit etwas Knoblauch und Zwiebel und legt es 6-8 Tage in saure Milch und Essig, nachdem man es gesalzen und mit Pfeffer bestreut hat, auch gibt man gleich in die Milch gehackte Zwiebeln, gelbe Rüben und Lorbeerblätter. Dann bräunt man das Fleisch mit Butter gut an, gibt etwas von der sauren Milch hinzu und läßt es darin gar schmoren. Dann nimmt man das Fleisch heraus, zieht die Sauce mit Sahne und Kraftmehl ab sodaß sie gut seimig ist und reibt etwas Muskatnuß d'ran. Giebt man der Sauce noch ein Glas Rothwein und Citronenscheiben, so ist sie ganz delikat. Diese Portion reicht für 12 Personen.

Frau Emilie Pfeiffer.

Labskaus. — (Eine deutsche Land- und Schiffskost.) Man nehme entweder frischgekochtes oder übriggebliebens Braten- und Suppenfleisch, und etwas geräuchertes Schweinefleisch. Nachdem man es von den Knochen frei gemacht hat, wird es fein gehackt. Man nehme die doppelte Portion Kartoffeln wie Fleisch, welche, nachdem sie gekocht, fein gestampft werden. Darnach schmore man eine feingeschnittene Zwiebel in Butter oder Bratenfett gar, gieße Fleischbrühe oder Bratensauce dazu und füge etwas feinen Pfeffer bei. Dann mische man Fleisch und Kartoffeln mit der Brühe gut durch und lasse es eben aufkochen und gebe nach Belieben noch ein Stück Butter dazu.

Meta Rahtjen.

Blinder Haase. Nimm zwei Pfund Rindfleisch und zwei Pfund fein gehacktes Schweinefleisch, vier Eier, eine fein geriebene Zwiebel, etwas fein gehackte Petersilie und nach Geschmack Muskatnuß, Pfeffer und Salz. Menge Alles tüchtig durcheinander, lege es in Form eines Haasen in eine Pfanne, bestreiche den Haasen tüchtig mit Butter und brate im Ofen 1½ Stunden. Kann auch kalt als Aufschnitt benutzt werden. Mit selbstgemachten Nudeln oder Maccaronis ist dieses ein vorzügliches Gericht.

Frau Marie Hassel
Richmond, Va.

Rehbraten. — Eine gut gehäutete Rehkeule reinigt man von dem Fett und spickt sie mit ¼ Pfund fettem Speck. In einer bedeckten Pfanne bratet man mit ¼ Pfund Butter eine Stunde. Dann giebt man Wasser dazu und begießt alle 10 Minuten. Das Fleisch muß 2 Stunden braten und dann fügt man 1 Pt. sauren Rahm mit Mehl verrührt hinzu, läßt es noch eine halbe Stunde braten und begießt recht oft, damit der Braten einen schönen braunen Glanz erhält. Man servirt mit Nudeln.

Agathe Liebig.

—24—

Hammelkeule wie Wild zubereitet. — Will man das Fleisch nicht in Essig legen, so darf es nicht zu frisch geschlachtet sein, da es sonst nicht mürbe wird. Die Keule wird gut geklopft, gehäutet, das Fett abgelöst und dann wie Hasen gespickt, mit Nelken und Nelken= pfeffer eingerieben und in Speck und Butter gelb gemacht. Man gibt schließlich Salz und süße Milch nach Geschmack dazu.

Mary Beesenmeyer.

———

Saure Zunge. — Für eine gute weichgekochte Zunge nimmt man einen Kochlöffel voll Butter und einen voll Mehl, bräunt dies, und fügt ¼ Pfund Mandeln und ¼ Pfund Rosinen dazu. Essig und Zucker nach Belieben. Vom Feuer genommen, giebt man noch ein Glas Wein zu, schneidet die Zunge fein und gießt die Sauce darüber

Emma Stein.

———

Ungarischer Guilacz. — 6 Pfd. mageres Rindfleisch schneidet man in kleine Würfel. Dann thut man in einen Topf je ½ Pfund Butter und Fett und läßt darin circa 2 Qt. geschnittene Zwiebeln leicht anbräunen, thut das zerschnittene Fleisch hinein, läßt es ziemlich gar werden, nachdem man es vorher gut gesalzen hat und gibt noch et= was Pfeffer und Lorbeerblätter hinzu. Dann giebt man so viel Fleisch= brühe zu als man Sauce haben will, zieht diese mit Mehl ab, gut sei= mig, würzt sie mit nicht zu wenig rothen Pfeffer und etwas Muskatnuß. Für 12 Personen.

Frau Pauline Goldammer.

———

Hammelschlegel mit Rahm=Sauce. — Ein guter, mürber Schlegel wird einige Tage in Essig gelegt und dann gut mit Butter oder Speck gebraten. Eine halbe Stunde vor dem Anrichten wird er entfettet und dann eine Tasse sauren Rahms darüber gegossen.

M. Schell.

ERNST HAUCK,

DEALER IN

Stoves, Tin and Hardware,

Bakers' Supplies,

ALSO MANUFACTURER OF

Tin, Copper and Sheet Iron Work,

383 Division Street,

Opp. Franklin St.

Roofing, Guttering and Jobbing done to order.

BEEF A LA MODE. — Take a shoulder piece, lay it in vinegar for 2 or 3 days with spices and onions. Before putting on the stove draw it with salt pork, brown a little piece of bacon, lay the meat in this and let it get brown, add your vinegar and spices with half a lemon and a crust of rye bread. Let this boil until tender. Before serving grate two ginger snaps, add to the vinegar and let it come to a boil.

MARGARET RAITHEL.

SPARE RIBS WITH APPLE DRESSING. — For dressing, use tart apples peeled and quartered, roll and tie the meat, pepper and salt and bake in oven. Serve with baked potatoes.

ELLA KORRER.

FILLET ROAST. — 3½ lbs. of fillet roast, draw with bacon, put in the pan with butter the size of an egg, season with pepper and salt, add one cup of cold water, put in a hot oven for one hour. When done, finish sauce by adding a little flour and boiling water.

CLARA STEIN.

VEAL ROAST. — Lay the meat in dripping pan, sprinkle with salt and pepper, and cover with a few pieces of butter and a slice of fat bacon ; then add an onion, a few cloves, a carrot, ½ cup water and ½ cup white wine. Baste freely. Roast in steady oven 1¼ hours. This is the way they roast veal in Switzerland.

AUGUSTA HAHL.

SCALLOPED MEAT. — This is made of any scraps or bits of good meat that happen to be left. Chop fine and have ready for each cup of meat one cup of stewed and seasoned tomatoes and one of bread crumbs. Butter a shallow pudding dish, sprinkle with part of crumbs. Then add part of meat, then the tomatoes, then the rest of meat, and then the rest of crumbs. Sprinkle with a spoonful of butter, broken into bits. Bake 20 or 30 minutes.

MAMIE GROSS.

JOHN HEIDE,

DEALER IN

Choice GROCERIES,

PROVISIONS, ETC.

378 WELLS STREET.

JOHN PH. STROH,

Bakery and Confectionery,

 **421 WELLS STREET.**

Orders for Wedding and Fancy Cakes
promptly attended to.

—28—

Gemüse.

Spinat. — Koche den Spinat gut, schütte das heiße Wasser ab und begieße 2 oder 3 mal mit kaltem. Drücke aus, verhacke mit einer Zwiebel und einem Stück Weißbrod, gieb etwas Fleischbrühe zu und koche langsam.

Karoline Roß.

Weiße Rüben. — Sie werden der Länge nach fein geschnitten. In eine Kasserole wird ein Stück Butter mit etwas Zucker leicht gebräunt. Man thut die Rüben hinein, dünstet sie weich, staubt sie mit Mehl, gibt etwas Fleischbrühe zu und kocht noch ein wenig.

A. Böckeler.

Nudeln mit Aepfeln. — Man kocht Hohlnudeln, die sogenannten Maccaroni in Salzwasser und in einem anderen Topf Aepfel mit Citronenschale, Zimmt und Zucker gar. Eine Auflaufschüssel wird mit Butter ausgestrichen und mit Zwieback bestreut. Die Hohlnudeln und Aepfel werden abwechselnd schichtweise eingelegt und kleine Stückchen Butter dazwischen gethan. Die obere Schicht muß aus Nudeln bestehen. Das Ganze wird mit Zwieback bestreut und mit 3 geschlagenen Eiern übergossen, dann eine Stunde in nicht zu heißem Ofen gebacken. Hat man kein frisches Obst, so kann man auch sehr gut die jetzt so ausgezeichneten gedörrten Aepfel verwenden.

Anna Ziehm.

—30—

Apfelreis. — Wasche 1 Tasse voll Reis, koche denselben in Wasser, ein Stückchen Butter, ganzen Zimmt und Citronenschale beinahe weich, salze nach Geschmack, füge 4 mittelgroße saure Aepfel, ½ Tasse gewaschene Corinthen und etwas Zucker hinzu, und lasse alles zusammen weich kochen. Man gibt gebratenes Fleisch dazu.

Louise Keiter.

Sauce zu Blumenkohl. — Man nehme 3 Eier, 1 Eßlöffel Mehl, schlage es gut zusammen, 2 Tassen voll Blumenkohl=Wasser ½ Tasse Essig und eine oz. Butter. Die Butter lasse man in einem Topf über gelindem Feuer zergehen, thue die Eier mit dem Mehl und Blumenkohl=Wasser und Essig hinzu, rühre beständig bis zum Kochen, nehme ½ Theelöffel voll Zucker, reibe etwas Muskatnuß und servire mit dem Blumenkohl. Diese Sauce eignet sich für Fisch und Hühner.

Alma Claussen.

Grüne Bohnen. — Die Bohnen werden gespalten, dann in Salzwasser weich gesotten. Hernach wird das Wasser abgegossen, einige Kochlöffel voll Mehl werden in Butter gelb geröstet, Zwiebeln und Petersilie daran gedämft, die Bohnen hinein gethan und dann gekocht.

F. D.

BUTTER OR WAX BEANS. - Cut the beans lengthwise in two or three strips. Boil until soft. Drain well, return to kettle, add milk, butter, and salt to suit taste.

EMMA RUDOWSKY.

COLD SLAW. — Chop one head of cabbage fine, mix it with one cup of vinegar, 1 teaspoonful of mustard, 2 tablespoonfuls of sugar, a small lump of butter, put it on the stove and let it come to a boil, let it cool, and then add 1 beaten egg and 1 teaspoonful of salt.

H. H.

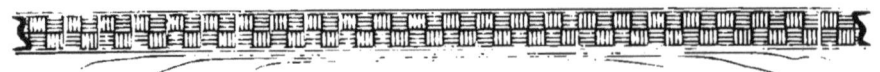

AT THE OLD RELIABLE

Union Tailoring Co.,

30 Clybourn Ave. 30

you can always obtain the best
value for your money.

All Wool Pants made to order from
upwards. **$4.00**

All Wool Suits from **$16.00**
upwards.

Overcoats in great variety also at low prices.

SATISFACTION GUARANTEED
IN EVERY INSTANCE.

Harry M. Brown.

MASHED POTATOES (WARMED OVER). — To two cupfuls of cold mashed potatoes add a half cupful of milk, a pinch of salt, a tablespoonful of flour, and two eggs beaten to a froth. Mix the whole until thoroughly light; then put into a pudding or vegetable dish, spread a little butter over the top, and bake a golden brown. The quality depends upon very thoroughly beating the eggs before adding them, so that the potato will remain light and porous after baking, similar to sponge cake.

C. E. M.

———

STEWED CABBAGE. — Take one head of cabbage, cut fine, one heaping tablespoonful flour, stir until brown, add 1 pint water, scant ½ cup vinegar, 1 heaping tablespoonful sugar, 1 large apple sliced and 1 onion, add a little salt. Boil about 40 minutes.

Mrs. G. C. SPOERER.

———

ASPARAGUS ON TOAST. — Tie two bunches of asparagus with soft string, cook in salt water until tender, have ready some slices of toast, butter while hot, drain the asparagus and arrange upon the toast. Take a pint of milk, 2 tablespoons of butter, salt to taste, boil 2 eggs hard, cut them in the milk, let it come to a boil and thicken with flour. Pour over the asparagus.

Mrs. M. HESSEMER.

DUCHESS POTATOES. — Take enough mealy potatoes to make a good dishful. Boil them dry, and while still hot they must be beaten with a silver fork. When they are fine and mealy, take two tablespoonfuls of cream, one of butter, salt and pepper to taste, and the beaten yolks of two eggs. Whip all these together until they are like cream. Mix in the whites of the eggs beaten to a froth. When the mixture is cold, cut in squares and put in a greased baking pan. Place them in rows, but do not have them touch. Brush over the tops and sides with white of the egg when they are brown, and bake until a nice brown.

IDA SCHMIDT.

———

FRIED PARSNIPS. — Scrape and cut lengthwise in slices a quarter of an inch thick. Boil until they are tender, then drain, dip in egg and rolled cracker, and fry a nice brown in butter or beef drippings.

MRS. NAPER.

———

EGG PLANT. — Pare and slice about ¼ inch thick, sprinkle salt over each piece and let stand two hours. Then wipe dry and dip in egg and flour or cracker and fry brown.

MRS. WEBSTER.

———

POTATO CROQUETTES. — Take mashed potatoes and season with salt, pepper and butter. Mix in the yolks of four or more eggs, as the quantity may require. Let it cool, then roll in shape, break in egg and cracker meal, and fry till brown.

MRS. NAPER.

———

—35—

—36—

COLD SLAW. — Beat two eggs, two tablespoonfuls of sugar, ½ teaspoonful of mustard, butter size of an egg, pepper and salt to taste. Pour a cup of hot vinegar over this, beat quickly to prevent curdling, and pour over the chopped cabbage.

EMMA SPRING.

CURLY CABBAGE. — Cut the cabbage in quarters, put in boiling salt water, boil until tender, take out and chop fine. Put in cup of milk or cream in porcelain lined kettle, stir in one tablespoonful of flour mixed with cream and tablespoonful butter, put in cabbage and boil 5 minutes; flavor with nutmeg.

OLGA KREMBS.

Salat.

Kartoffel Salat. — Man kocht Kartoffeln in der Schale, zieht sie ab und schneidet sie in recht dünne Scheiben. Dann gibt man dazu fein geschnittene Zwiebeln, Pfeffer, Salz und gutes Speiseöl. Sodann kocht man Essig, mischt ihn zur Hälfte mit Fleischbrühe, gießt es heiß über die Kartoffeln, mengt es gut durcheinander, läßt es ein paar Stunden stehen und servirt.

Frau Emilie Pfeiffer.

H. Stadelmann,

Merchant ∴ Tailor,

220 North State Street.

For Pure Teas, Coffees, Etc.

go to the

BELL TEA CO.,

446 LARRABEE ST.

Fred Knauf, Prop. & Manager,

Try our Java Coffee. All Mail orders promptly attended to.

CHICKEN SALAD. — Boil together 1 teaspoonful sugar, ½ pepper, ⅓ mustard, 1 salt, 1 cup vinegar and 1 tablespoon butter. Stir this boiling mixture into the yolks of 10 eggs and let it cool. Then add cream until it becomes thin, cut chicken and add above with 1 teaspoonful celery (celery salt) or stick celery, cut like chicken.

TILLIE RUTISHAUSER.

SALAD DRESSING. — Two tablespoons mustard, 1 tablespoon sugar, 1 teaspoon salt, boiling water enough to make thick paste, 3 eggs well beaten, 1 cup cream or milk, ¾ cup melted butter, 1 cup vinegar. Mix in earthen dish, set in boiling water and cook until it begins to thicken.

EMILIE HOFFMAN.

HAM SALAD. — Take cold boiled ham, fat and lean, chop until thoroughly mixed and the pieces size of peas. Then add an equal quantity of celery cut fine, or if this is out of season substitute lettuce, line a dish thickly with lettuce leaves and fill with the chopped ham and celery. Pour over this a cream salad dressing.

IDA STIEFEL.

HERRING SALAD. — Take four herrings, two boiled beets, two apples, two boiled eggs, two onions, a little boiled or roasted meat, two pickles and two small boiled potatoes. Chop fine like hash and season with vinegar to taste.

HELEN MILLER.

E. Muelhoefer & Bro.,

UNDERTAKERS,

112-114 Clybourn Avenue.

Bettfedern!

Chas. Emmerich & Co.

175-181 S. Canal St., Cor. Jackson.

nahe der Brücke.

Beim Kauf von Federn außerhalb unseres Hauses bitten wir auf die
Marke von C. E. & CO. zu achten, welche alle
von uns kommenden Sachen tragen.

CHICKEN SALAD. — Boil large chicken until tender. When cold pick to pieces, add 6 stalks celery cut fine. Dressing: Take 1 pt. cream, put in oatmeal strainer, add 1 teaspoonful mustard dissolved in cream, yolk of 6 eggs, let boil, stirring to keep from curdling. When cold mix part of dressing with chicken, add salt and vinegar; a little broth improves the taste. The remainder of the dressing pour over your salad.

Mrs. CHAS. E. REHM.

VEAL SALAD. — Two lbs. roast veal and equal quantity cabbage, two stalks celery, 3 hard boiled eggs. Chop cabbage, celery and whites of eggs together, then add the veal, also chopped. For dressing take yolks, celery, salt and cayenne pepper to taste, 1 tablespoonful mustard, vinegar to moisten.

KATIE SCHMIDT, Toledo, Ohio.

Kartoffel Salat. — *Zu ¼ Pf. gekochter und in Scheiben geschnittener Kartoffeln nimm ¼ Tasse Essig, ¼ Tasse Wasser, 1 feingehackte Zwiebel, zerstoßenen Pfeffer, ein wenig Salz, 2 Löffel ausgebratenes Fett von gekochtem Schinken, oder Butter, oder 1 Löffel Salatöl, und 1 Löffel Zucker. Man rührt Alles gut durcheinander. Am besten ist es wenn die Kartoffeln bei'm Zubereiten noch warm sind.

Louise Reiter.

—42—

SWEET SOUR BEANS. — ½ bu. wax beans, 2 qts. vinegar, 3 lbs. sugar and stick cinnamon. Boil beans tender in salt water and drain. In the meantime heat vinegar, sugar and cinnamon, pour boiling hot over the beans.

DORA HAAKE.

LOBSTER SALAD. — Boil a large lobster in slightly salted water rapidly for 15-20 minutes. When done it will be of a bright color and should be removed; if boiled too long it will be tough. When cold, crack the claws, twist off head—which is used in garnishing—split body lengthwise and pick out meat, saving the coral. Cut up large head of lettuce, lay on dish and lobster on this, putting coral around the outside. For dressing, take yolks of 4 eggs, beat well, add 4 tablespoonfuls salad oil, dropping it in very slowly, beating it all the time. Then add a bit of salt, cayenne pepper, ½ teaspoonful of mustard and 2 tablespoonfuls of vinegar. Pour this over the lobster just before serving.

Mrs. A. M. HOFMAN.

CHICKEN SALAD. — Boil chicken tender, chop moderately fine the whites of 12 hard boiled eggs and the chicken, add equal quantity of chopped celery, mash yolks fine, add 1 teaspoonful mustard, 2 tablespoons butter, 2 of sugar, pepper and salt to taste, ½ cup of good vinegar. Pour over chicken and mix thoroughly.

Mrs. A. HUMMEL.

John Kranz,

✳✳✳ *Confectioner,*

78-80 State Street,

All kinds of Fresh Candies made daily.

Try our delicious Buttercups, Molasses Candy, Caramels, Etc.

R. LOTHHOLZ & Co.,

Wholesale and Retail

Frisches & Gesalzenes Fleisch

71 NORTH CLARK ST.

Telephone North-539.

Schinken, Speck, Schmalz, ꝛc.

Bologna u. andere Sorten Wurst von feinster Qualität.

—44—

CHICKEN SALAD. — Boil chicken until tender. When cold cut in small pieces, add about as much celery cut fine, 3 hard boiled eggs sliced, thoroughly mixed with the other ingredients. For dressing: Put saucepan on stove with 1 pt. vinegar, beat 2-3 eggs with 1 tablespoonful of ground mustard, 1 teaspoonful of black pepper, 1 teaspoonful salt and a little sugar. Mix well and pour slowly into the vinegar until it thickens, add butter size of an egg last. Be careful not to cook too long or the egg will curdle. A little lemon juice will improve it. Garnish with slices of lemon.

MARY KURZ.

MIXED SALAD. — 1 qt. wax beans, finely sliced, boil in salt water until tender, drain. When cold add two medium sized green cucumbers, finely sliced, then pour over ½ pt. sweet cream, pepper, salt and vinegar to taste.

Mrs. J. BODMER.

HERRING SALAD. — 6 herrings, same amount of veal, small cup of pickles, same of beets, 4 hard boiled eggs. Cut all this in dice shapes. Dressing: Take milkings of two herrings, mash well, add 1 egg, 1 tablespoon salad oil, 1 teaspoon each of pepper and mustard, small onion grated, vinegar to taste and mix thoroughly.

H. AHRENS.

45 –

HUGO T. PETERSEN,
President.

EMIL EITEL,
Secretary and Treasurer.

Universal Pot Lifter Co.

PATENTED.

Office : 316 Chamber of Commerce,

Telephone Main-4873.

CARL EITEL, MANAGER.

D. E. REIMERS,

DEALER IN

Dry Goods and Notions,

219 NORTH AVENUE, COR. ORCHARD.

Gemischter Wintersalat. — 3 Theile in der Schale weich gekochte Kartoffeln, 1 Theil saure Aepfel, 1 Theil rothe Rüben, 1 Theil eingemachte Gurken. Alles dies zu feinen Scheiben geschnitten, mit einer gut gerührten Sauce von reichlich Oel, etwas saurer Sahne, Essig, Pfeffer und Salz vorsichtig durchgemengt, daß die Scheiben ganz bleiben. In eine Salatiere angerichtet, ein Kranz von Kornsalat mit Oel, Essig und Salz vermischt, ringsum gelegt und denselben mit nicht ganz hart gekochten Eiern, welche zu 8 Theilen geschnitten werden, schrägliegend verziert. Es wird kaltes Fleisch oder Häring dazu gegeben.

Lina Buenneke.

CHICKEN SALAD. One 4 pound chicken, boiled until tender. When cold, chop meat very fine; 2 stalks celery chopped fine Make a liquor of yolks of 3 eggs, 2 tablespoons of salad oil, 1 tablespoon of butter, season to taste with salt, pepper and vinegar. Boil and pour over the chicken.

Mrs. A. MAHNKEN.

Klöße.

Leber-Klöße. — Ein Pfund gehackte Kalbsleber, Pfeffe und Salz nach Geschmack, ein wenig Majoran und fein geriebene Zwie bel, 3 Eier, ¼ Weißbrot eingeweicht und ausgedrückt. Man mischt mi Mehl zu einem Teig den man mit dem Löffel ausstechen kann, läßt die Klöße gut gar kochen, gießt etwas gebratenen Speck darüber und gibt gutes Sauerkraut dazu.

Frau Ittel.

FLOUR

makes

More Bread

Better Bread

Whiter Bread

than any other Flour

—

Daily Product of the Pillsbury Mills 15,500 Barrels.

Sold by all Grocers.

Leber-Knödel.   Brod fein geschnitten, in Milch eingeweicht und dann gut ausgedrückt. Kalbsleber fein gewiegt und Zwiebel, Petersilie, Majoran, Salz, ein wenig Citronenschale und ein Stückchen Nierenfett oder Mark, 3 bis 4 Eier, alles gut vermengt, kleine Knö-
bel geformt und in der Fleischsuppe fertig gekocht.

M. Schell.

———

Leber-Klöße. — 2 Pfund Leber und ¼ Pfund Rindsfett
zusammen fein gehackt. Semmel oder Weißbrot in Wasser geweicht u
fest ausgedrückt. 3 Eier, 1 Tasse Mehl, Petersilie, Muskatnuß, Pfeffer und Salz. Gut gemischt, Klöße gemacht und 20 Minuten in Salzwasser gekocht.

Frau Louise Schmidt.

———

Leber-Klöße. — Die Leber wird gewaschen, gehäutet und
geschabt. Einige Zwiebeln werden in ¼ Pfund Nierenfett gedämpft.
Zu 1 Pfund Leber nimmt man 2 Wecken, die eine weicht man ein und
drückt sie dann aus, die andere reibt man. Dies thut man dann in eine
Schüssel mit Salz, Pfeffer, Majoran und Muskatnuß, schlägt 2 Eier
darein, rührt die Masse tüchtig um und streut so viel Mehl darüber, daß
es einen steifen Teig gibt. Man formt die Klöße mit einem Löffel und
läßt sie in Salzwasser kochen. Sie sind gar sobald sie inwendig eine
weißliche Farbe bekommen. Man richtet an mit in Butter geröstetem
Brod oder gedämpften Zwiebeln.

Frau P. Helfenstein.

Kartoffel = Klöße. — Die mit der Schale in Salzwasser nicht ganz weich gekochten Kartoffeln werden geschält und wenn ganz kalt geworden, gerieben. Zu 5 Suppentellern geriebener Kartoffeln nimmt man 1 Suppenteller geriebenes altes Weißbrod, ¼ oz. ausgelassenen Speck, ⅛ Muskatnuß, 6 Eier (das Weiße zu Schaum geschlagen) 1 Kochlöffel Mehl, 2 Theelöffel Salz. Man rollt handdicke Klöße, bestreut sie mit Mehl und kocht etwa 15 Minuten in Salzwasser, Man richtet an mit brauner Butter und gibt gekochtes Obst dazu.

Anna Hochstedt.

———

Kartoffel = Klöße. — Die Kartoffeln werden am Tage vor dem Gebrauch in der Schale in Salzwasser abgekocht, dann geschält und gerieben. Zu 3 Theilen Kartoffeln 1 Thl. geriebenes Weißbrod in Butter gebräunt. Auf einen Suppenteller voll ⅛ Eßl. Mehl, 2 Eier (das Weiße zu Schaum geschlagen), 1 Eßlöffel gebräunte Butter. Gut vermengt, Klöße gemacht, 10 bis 15 Minuten in Salzwasser gekocht, braune Butter darüber und gekochtes Obst als Zugabe.

N. N.

———

DAMPFNUDELN. — 1 qt. of milk, 1 cent's worth of compressed yeast, enough flour to thicken; let rise. Then add 1 tablespoonful butter, 2 eggs, pinch of salt, make into rolls and put on board to rise. Put into large skillet 1 cup water, 1 teaspoonful butter and pinch of salt. When boiling, cover bottom of skillet with a layer of the rolls, cover tightly and let boil for 15 minutes or until dry, without uncovering. Serve with stewed prunes or any desired fruit, or with potato soup.

Minnie E. Jacobs.

CASPAR HAHN,

DEALER IN

Paints, Oils, Glass, Wall Paper

and Window Shades.

35 & 37 CLYBOURN AVE.

Carpenter Work at short notice.

Kartoffel = Klöße. — 2 Qt. Kartoffeln, geschält, gekocht und dann fein gerührt. Etwas Salz und mit heißer Milch zu einem dicken Brei gerührt, ½ Pfund Kartoffelmehl, 2 Eier und dann gut ver= rührt – und zwar so heiß als nur möglich, weil dann die Klöße schnell kochen und locker werden. Ehe die Kartoffeln gerührt werden, röste kleine Würfel Weißbrod in Butter oder Speck und thue in jeden Kloß, der so groß sein darf wie etwa eine schöne Orange, 5 bis 6 derselben und drücke ihn dann gut zu. Laß die Klöße nicht zu lange kochen. Sie schmecken sehr gut und man gibt sie mit irgend einem Braten.

M. Herrmann.

———

Servietten = Kloß. — Ein Laib Weißbrod in Milch einge= weicht, 6 Eier, 1 geriebene Muskatnuß, etwas Salz zu einem Teig ge= rührt und in eine große Serviette gebunden, wobei man aber Raum lassen muß zum „Aufgehen" des Kloßes. Man thut Letzteren dann in einen Topf siedenden Wassers und läßt ihn ½ Stunde kochen. Dabei sieht man öfters nach, daß er nicht anbrennt. Man gebrauche einen recht großen Topf. Serviere mit dieser Sauce: 1 Eßlöffel voll heißer Butter, 1 Pt. Wasser, ½ Tasse Essig kocht man zusammen und rührt dann ½ Tasse Syrup und zwei Lorbeerblätter hinein. Man schlägt die Masse durch ein Sieb, gießt sie wieder in den Topf zurück, verdickt mit 2 Theelöffel aufgelöster Kornstärke und läßt ein paar Minuten kochen.

Caroline Emmel.

———

Schwammklößchen. — 1 Laib Brod gerieben, 2 Eier, Salz, Muskatnuß, in einen Topf gethan, gut mit heißer Fleisch=Suppe am Feuer verrührt, ein paar Minuten kochen und dann anrichten.

A. Böckeler.

GEO. SIEGFRIED

Ladies Hair Dressing and Manicure Parlors,

Manufacturer of all kinds of

HUMAN HAIR GOODS.

Room 42,
78 STATE STREET.

I. M. CARDY,

Dry Goods and Millinery

Cor. Halsted St. & Garfield Ave.

Dehmlow Bros.

Chemical Cleaning and Steam Dye House,

Works and Office, 543 Lincoln Ave.,

Branch, 954 N. Halsted St.

G. R. WOLFF,

Watchmaker and Jeweler,

950 N. Halsted Street.

Schwammklößchen. — ¼ Pfund Butter schaumig gerührt, 3 Eier, Salz, Muskatnuß, Mehl nach Bedarf, gut verrührt, mit einem Kaffeelöffel eingelegt, ¼ Stunde in guter Fleischsuppe gekocht.

M. Schell.

Gries = Klöße. — Koche 1 Pt. Milch ab, mache mit Gries einen steifen Teig und gieb einen guten Theelöffel Butter, Salz und Muskatnuß dazu. Ist die Masse ein wenig abgekühlt rühre 4 bis 5 Eier, eins nach dem andern hinein, stich mit einen Theelöffel Klößchen ab und lege sie in kochende Fleischbrühe.

Rosina Gottmanshausen.

Saure Fleischklöße. — Nimm zu 1 Pfund gehacktem Schweinefleisch 1 Tasse geriebenes Weißbrod, 1 Ei, 1 feingehackte Zwiebel, ein wenig allspice Pfeffer und Salz. Rühre gut durch und mache Klöße daraus. Dann löste 1 gehäuften Eßlöffel Mehl in 1 Eßlöffel Fett, gieße unter beständigem Rühren 3 Tassen Wasser dazu bis die Sauce schön „eben" ist, salze nach Geschmack, gieb zu, Gewürz, Nelken, Lorbeer, 2 bis 3 Eßlöffel Essig, etwas Zucker und dann lege die Klöße hinein und koche 10 Minuten.

Louise Reiter.

POTATO DUMPLINGS. — Boil some potatoes and grate them. Peal and grate some raw potatoes, put in a bag, press out all the juice, put in a dish, add salt and flour, scald with hot water, and then mix in the boiled potatoes. Dip hands in cold water while making dumplings, put in boiling water for ½ hour. Serve with small squares of bread fried in butter.

Clara Detmer.

Marfflöße. — Man nehme ein wallnußdickes Stück Mark und reibe es zu Sahne, schlage zwei ganze Eier, etwas Salz Muskat= nuß und 2 Eßlöffel kaltes Wasser mit zwei fein geriebenen Semmeln hinzu und rühre alles miteinander gut durch; forme mit der Hand Klöß= chen daraus und lege sie in kochenden Bouillon; sollten dieselben zu weich sein, so thue noch ein wenig geriebene Semmel dazu. Feingeschnittene Petersilie verbessert den Geschmack der Klößchen.

Frau Henrici.

———

Klöße von Rindfleisch.—Es wird ein ¼ Pf. beefsteak recht fein gehackt, alles Sehnige entfernt, dann dazu: ⅛ Pfund Butter zu Sahne gerührt, 2 Eidotter, eingeweichtes und ausgedrücktes Milchbrod, Muskatnuß, Salz und zuletzt den Schaum von einem Eiweiß. Die Masse muß weich sein aber doch gut zusammen halten. Man sticht mit einem Löffel ab und kocht 5 Minuten in der Suppe.

Helene Lüpsch.

———

POTATO DUMPLINGS. — Boil 1 doz. potatoes; when soft, mash fine as soon as cold, add 6 tablespoonfuls flour, 1 table-spoon baking powder, 1 of melted butter, 4 eggs beaten light, salt and nutmeg to taste, mix well, form into balls and fill with small squares of buttered toast, put into boiling water which has been well salted, and boil 15 minutes. Serve with fricasse or pot roast.

Mrs. C. W. Haubold.

C. Leupold & Co.,

Dealers in

Staple & Fancy Groceries,

Candies, Cigars and Tobacco,

1295 North Halsted St.

Fleischklöße mit Rahmsauce. — Man nimmt 1 Pfund gehacktes Fleisch, halb Schweine und halb Rindfleisch, (läßt man etwas fettes Schweinefleisch mit hacken so bleiben die Klöße saftiger), lasse ein Weißbrödchen in Wasser aufweichen, drücke aus, lege es zu dem Fleisch, schlage ein Ei hinein, etwas feingeschnittene Zwiebel, Salz und Pfeffer, rühre alles gut durcheinander und forme eigroße runde Klöße. Koche sie dann in soviel kochendem Wasser, daß sie beinahe davon bedeckt werden, mit 2 Lorbeerblättern, paar Nelken, etwas ganzen Pfeffer und paar Zwiebelscheiben beinahe gar. Verrühre sodann in 1 Tasse voll dicken sauren Rahm 3 Theelöffel Mehl und gieße denselben unter beständigem Rühren zu den kochenden Klößen, füge ein Stückchen Butter hinzu und lasse Alles zusammen tüchtig durchkochen. Man kann auch etwas Essig zu dem Rahm gießen, sollte derselbe nicht genügend sauer sein. Salz nach Geschmack.

Lina Schwabe.

Apfelklöße. — 1 Tasse gehacktes Rindsfett, 3 Tassen Mehl, gut vermischt, 1 Theelöffel Salz, rühre mit kalten Wasser an und mache Teig steif genug zum Ausrollen, mache Klöße mit ¼ Apfel, ein wenig Zucker, lege in kochendes Wasser und koche 20 Minuten.

Sauce: 1 Tasse Zucker, ¼ Tasse Butter, rühre gut zusammen; 1 Pt. kochendes Wasser mit ein wenig Mehl; gieße dazu ¼ Weinglas Brandy oder Wein.

Frau G. Heppe.

Käse-Keulchen. — Mit 1 Tasse lauwarme Milch und 1 ct. Hefe macht man einen weichen Teig und läßt ihn stehen bis er Blasen zieht. Dann: 1 Eßlöffel Butter, 2 Eßlöffel Schmierkäse, 1 Ei, 2 Eßlöffel Zucker, ¼ Tasse Corinthen, ¼ Tasse Milch. Rühre das Ganze mit etwas Mehl zusammen und laß es gähren. Theile es dann in kleine Stücke und laß nochmals gähren. Nach etwa einer Stunde sind sie fertig um in kochenden Fett bereitet zu werden.

Maria Conrad.

DUMPLING. — ½ loaf white bread cut in thin slices, trim off crusts, soak in milk ½ hour, add 2 well-beaten eggs, salt, pinch of nutmeg, tablespoonful melted butter, ¼ lb farina, mix lightly, tie in a cloth, boil 1 hour in salt water.

Marguerite Raithel.

ALMOND TORTE. — 1½ cups sugar, 2 cups of grated stale white bread or biscuit crumbs, 9 eggs, the whites beaten separately, 1 teaspoon of cinnamon, 1 teaspoon baking powder, ½ lb. of sweet almonds chopped fine. Do not blanch the almonds.

Mrs. Fred Heide, Jr.

FRUIT CAKE. — 1 lb. of powdered sugar, 1 lb. of flour, ¾ lb. of butter, 8 eggs, ½ lb. currants washed, picked over and dredged, ½ lb. of raisins, seeded and chopped, then dredged, ¼ lb. citron cut into small pieces, 1 teaspoonful nutmeg, 1 teaspoonful cinnamon, 1 cup of best brandy, cream, butter and sugar, add eggs, spice, flour, the fruit and brandy last.

Therese Maier, Baltimore.

DELICATE CAKE. — 2 cups sugar, 3 cups flour, ¾ cups sweet milk, whites of 6 eggs, ½ cup butter, 1 teaspoon cream of tartar, ½ teaspoonful of soda, flavor with lemon.

Etta Herbster.

WIND. — 4 eggs, 4 tablespoons of cream, butter the size of an egg, roll thin, cut in small slices, twist them and fry in hot lard, then sprinkle with sugar.

Mrs. J. J. A.

APPLE TORTE. — Dough: ¾ cups sugar, 3 eggs, a little lemon peel grated, 1 teaspoon baking powder, ¼ cup milk, flour to make a stiff dough. Line large pan with this and fill with sliced apples. Pour custard over this and bake very slow until custard and apples are done. Custard: 6 eggs, 1½ cups sugar, beat well, 1½ cups sour cream.

Mrs. W. Apfel.

————

BREAD TORTE. — 1 lb. sugar, 1½ cups grated bread, moistened with wineglass of red wine, 16 eggs, small piece citron, ½ lb. almonds chopped fine, 1 teaspoon cloves, 2 teaspoons cinnamon, 2 tablespoons chocolate, 1 teaspoon baking powder, beat ½ hour. When baked and cold, pour 1 wineglassful of white wine over the layers and spread jelly between.

Ida Koch, Toledo.

————

CHOCOLATE CAKE. — ½ cup butter, 2 cups sugar, ¾ cup sweet milk, 2½ cups flour, whites of 8 eggs, one teaspoonful cream tartar, ½ teaspoonful soda. Bake in shallow pans. Frosting: Whites of 3 eggs, 3 tablespoonfuls of sugar and 1 tablespoonful of grated chocolate (confectioner's) to one egg, put the cake together with the frosting, then frost the top with the same.

Emma Wurster.

CHOCOLATE CAKE. — 1½ cups of sugar, ½ cup of butter, ½ cup of milk, 1¾ cups of flour, ¼ lb. of Baker's chocolate, 3 eggs and 2 teaspoonfuls of baking powder. Scrape the chocolate fine and add five tablespoonfuls of sugar and three tablespoonfuls of boiling water, stirring over the fire till smooth and glossy. Beat the butter to a cream, add the sugar, then stir in the chocolate and the eggs well beaten. Then add milk, flour and baking powder. This can be used as layer or loaf cake.

Mrs. T. F. John, New Albany.

HICKORY NUT CAKE. — Two cups of sugar, one cup of butter, stir to a cream; whites of six eggs beaten stiff, one-fourth cup of milk, three cups of flour, two heaping teaspoonfuls of baking powder, one coffee cup of nut-meats; bake in a loaf.

Bertha Heuser.

CHOCOLATE CAKE. —Two cups sugar, one cup butter, beaten to a cream, add the yolks of five eggs, one cup milk. Sift or mix well together five cups of flour with two heaping teaspoonfuls of baking powder, flavor with lemon, then add the whites of three eggs, beaten to a stiff froth. Custard for same: Melt 1 tablespoonful chocolate. Take a half cup of pulverized sugar, add two tablespoonfuls of water, allow it to come to a boil, beat the whites of two eggs to a stiff froth, stir the syrup into this while hot. Then add three tablespoonfuls of chocolate and mix well and set aside to cool.

Frances Zschuppe.

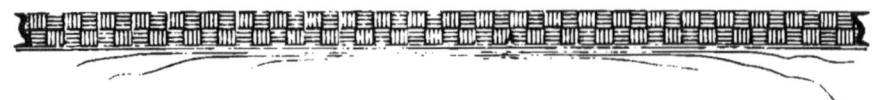

★ Engraved Visiting Cards

Wedding Invitations and Announcements, Engagement Cards, Fine Writing Paper with Monograms, Address and Crests Embossed in Colors and Bronzes.

ONLY THE FINEST WORK AT MODERATE PRICES.
MARKING ON JEWELRY AND SILVERWARE.

Wm. Freund & Sons,

Engravers on Steel, Copper and Jewelry.

155 STATE STREET, Top Floor.

Establ. 1865.

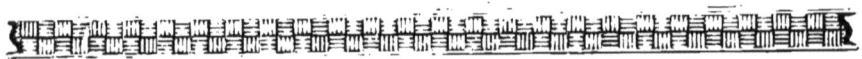

CHOCOLATE CAKE. — 1 cup pulverized sugar, 1 doz. eggs, 1 cup of bitter chocolate, 1 tablespoonful of cinnamon, 1 teaspoonful of ground cloves, 1½ cups flour and 1 teaspoonful of Price's baking powder.

Mrs. Fred Buscher.

———

BRANDY BRETZELS. — The yolks of six eggs boiled hard, one lb. of butter, ¼ lb. sugar, 1 lb. flour, ½ cup brandy and baking powder.

* *

——— ——

BUTTER BRETZELS. — 1 lb. flour, ½ lb. butter, ¼ lb. sugar, 1 egg, 1 yolk, 1 tablespoonful of cream, a little grated lemon peel, 1 teaspoonful baking powder.

M. Kiessling.

.

———

WALNUT WAFERS. — 1 cup walnut meats, chopped fine, 1 cup sugar, 1 tablespoon of flour, 1 egg. Dropped very small on tins. Bake in quick oven.

Louisa D. Sonnenschein.

WALNUT CAKE. — 2 cups of sugar, whites of 3 eggs, butter size of an egg, teaspoonful baking powder, 2 cups of flour, 1 cup of chopped walnuts. Bake ¾ of an hour in moderate oven.

Anna Dehlinger.

HICKORY NUT CAKES. — One cup butter, 2 cups sugar, whites of 7 eggs, yolks of 2, 1 cup milk, 3 cups flour, 3 teaspoonfuls Price's baking powder, 1 cup of chopped hickory nuts.

Lizzie Yahnke.

ALMOND CAKES. — 1 lb. shelled almonds, 1 oz. of citron, 1 lemon, whites of 6 eggs, 1 lb. powdered sugar, 2 tablespoons of flour. Chop the almonds and citron fine, add the juice and rind of lemon and the powdered sugar; beat the whites and mix lightly to the above. Last of all add the flour. Drop from a teaspoon to a buttered pan.

Katherine Wissler., Chillicothe, O.

FRUIT CAKE. — 2 lbs. raisins, 2 lbs. currants, 1 lb. butter, ¼ lb. citron, 1 cup molasses, ½ teaspoon soda, 1 cup coffee, 8 eggs, 1 teaspoon of all kinds of spices, 6 tablespoons brandy, 3 teaspoons baking powder, flour enough to thicken. Sift flour and baking powder together. Bake 3 hours.

Mrs. Rosa Bonn.

A Perfect Baking Powder.

The constantly growing demand for Dr. Price's Cream Baking Powder, the standard cream of tartar powder for forty years, is due to two causes.

FIRST:—The extreme care exercised by the manufacturers to make it perfectly pure, uniform in quality, and of greatest leavening power.

SECOND:—Recent investigations expose the fact that certain brands of baking powder contain ammonia and that still others contain alum. The unscrupulous manufacturers are being found out, and consumers are giving them a wide berth.

Nothing is left to chance in the manufacture of Dr. Price's Cream Baking Powder. Chemists are employed to test every ingredient as to purity and strength. Hence; its marvelous purity and uniformity. Each can is like every other. It never disappoints. The BEST is ALWAYS the CHEAPEST.

Dr. Price's Cream Baking Powder is reported by all authorities as free from Ammonia, Alum, or any other adulterant. In fact, the purity of this ideal baking powder has never been questioned.

SUGAR COOKIES MOLDED IN DIFFERENT FORMS. -- 2 lbs. flour, 1 lb. powdered sugar, 1 lb. butter, 2 teaspoonfuls saleratus, 4 eggs, 1 teaspoonful cinnamon. Rub butter and sugar together to a cream, then add 4 eggs one at a time, beating a few minutes after adding each. Mix saleratus with flour. Work the entire ingredients to a stiff dough Let stand 24 hours in a cold place, then ready to mold into different forms. Dip in egg and sugar before baking.

Mrs. K. Stiefel.

———

ORANGE CAKE. ---- 2 cups sugar, 2½ cups flour, ¼ cup water, 3 large teaspoons baking powder, yolks of five (5) eggs, whites of 12 eggs, grated rind and juice of 1 large orange. Bake in pans as for jelly cake. Put together as follows: Beat yolks and whites separately, put sugar and yolks together, after that water and orange, lastly flour with baking powder. Make quite a stiff frosting of the 3 remaining whites and powdered sugar, then add the whole of the grated rind and a little more than half the juice of another orange. Frost between each layer.

Anna J. G. Sonnenschein.

———

EXCELLENT APPLE CAKE. ---- One cup sugar, 1½ cups flour, 1 egg, butter size of an egg, 1 cup sour milk, ¼ teaspoonful soda, put sliced apples on top, and sugar and cinnamon.

Mrs. Naper.

(Geht nicht nach)

J. H. FRANKE & CO.,

The North Side Fair

283 & 285 North Ave.

nahe Larrabee Straße,

dem einzigen und größten Geschäfte seiner Art auf der Nordseite,

außer Ihr wollt die besten Waaren

für das wenigste Geld haben.

Telephone North-374.

JOHN G. ROLAND,

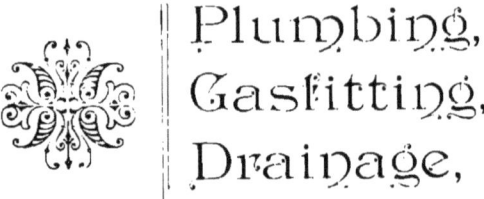 Plumbing,
Gasfitting,
Drainage,

952 North Halsted Street.

MACARONI. ---- To the stiff beaten whites of six eggs add one pound of powdered sugar and beat well. Then add one pound of prepared almond paste, chopped fine, and work this real well. Lastly, add two heaping teaspoonfuls of flour. Drop in small doses and bake in a slow oven.

Clara Kappes.

SILVER CAKE. --- ½ lb. sugar, ½ lb. flour, ¼ lb. butter, the whites of 7 eggs beaten to a stiff froth. Flavor with peach or almond extract. Bake and ice.

Amanda M. Andresen.

LIGHT FRUIT CAKE. --- Nine eggs, 1 lb. sugar, 1 lb. butter, 1 lb. flour, 1 lb. raisins, 1 lb. currants, ½ lb. citron, 1½ teaspoonfuls of Price's baking powder, one or two glasses of brandy.

Bertha Veesenmeyer.

FANCY DOUGHNUTS. ---- 2 cups of flour, 2 cups of water, 1 cup of butter, 5 eggs, 1 tablespoonful sugar, rind of a lemon. Let the water and butter boil. Then put in flour gradually and stir it until it is dry and does not stick to the kettle. Take it from the fire and stir in one egg, rind of lemon and sugar. After it has cooled somewhat stir in the remainder of eggs, one at a time. Beat it hard. Drop half a tablespoonful at a time into very hot lard. When done roll in sugar and cinnamon.

Annie Hoffman.

TILDEN CAKE. — One cup of butter, two cups pulverized sugar, one of sweet milk, three cups of flour, half cup corn starch, four eggs, two teaspoonfuls of baking powder, two teaspoonfuls of lemon extract. This can be baked in layers.

K. Lipsch.

ALMOND CAKE. — 1 pound of almonds, one lb. of pulverized sugar, 1 doz. of eggs, ½ cup of flour; stir one hour.

L. G. Haubold.

CHOCOLATE CAKE. - - 4 eggs, 2 cups sugar, 1 cup butter, 1 cup sweet milk, 3 cups flour, 3 teaspoonfuls baking powder, 2 teaspoons vanilla; heat well, divide into equal parts, and into one of these grate a cake of sweet chocolate. Bake in layers, spread with custard, alternately light and dark.

Mrs. R. C. Rudowsky.

WHITE FRUIT CAKE. — One cup butter, 2 cups of sugar, 1¼ cups of milk, 3 cups of flour, 2 teaspoonfuls of Price's baking powder, whites of 5 eggs, one grated cocoanut, one lb. blanched and chopped almonds, ½ lb. sliced citron.

Lydia John, Trenton, Ill.

Brown Stone Front. — 1 cup sugar, ½ cup butter, 3 eggs, ½ cup sweet milk with .teaspoon of soda dissolved in it. 2½ cups flour, ½ cake Baker's chocolate, ¾ cup milk, 1 cup sugar, yolk of 1 egg, to be cooked until thickened and added to the above when cold. Bake solid or in layers. If in layers, put together with boiled frosting, chocolate icing or any preferred way.

Miss Jacobs.

Sand Cake. — Yolks of 12 eggs, 1 lb. well sifted potato flour, 1 lb. sugar, 1 lb. butter, lastly the whites well beaten. Flavor with vanilla, put on well buttered paper and bake in moderate oven.

M. Pilling.

Marble Spice Cake. — Light: 1 cup sugar, ½ cup butter, ½ cup milk, 2 cups flour, whites of 3 eggs and 1½ teaspoonfuls of Dr. Price's Baking Powder. Dark: ½ cup brown sugar, ½ cup molasses, ¼ cup butter, ¼ cup milk, 2 cups flour, yolks of 3 eggs, 1½ teaspoonfuls baking powder and 3 teaspoonfuls of mixed spices.. Put batter into loaf pan and bake in a moderate oven.

Millie Schmidt, Toledo, O.

Fruit Cake. — One lb. raisins, one lb. currants, one lb. brown sugar, 4 eggs, 1 cup sour cream, ¼ lb. citron, 1 glass wine, 1 teaspoonful cinnamon, ½ teaspoonful ground cloves, 1 teaspoonful soda and 4 cups flour.

Mrs. Olbert.

78

PEPPER NUTS. — 6 yolks and 2 whites of eggs, 1 lb. white sugar, 1 pint of flour, 1 teaspoonful of hartshorn salt, 1 teaspoonful cloves, ½ teaspoonful allspice, 1 of pepper and ½ of nutmeg, 2 tablespoonfuls citron. Bake in a slow oven.

Minnie Eckebrecht.

CREAM CAKE. — 1 cup sugar, 1 tablespoonful butter, 1 egg, 1 cup milk, 2 cups of flour, 1 teaspoonful baking powder, flavor to taste, and a little salt. Cream for filling: 1 cup of milk, stir while boiling, 1 egg, ½ cup of sugar, ¼ cup of corn starch, a pinch of salt and a little extract; stir in the boiling milk until thick.

H. K.

LEBKUCHEN. — ½ gallon molasses, 1 lb. lard, 1 lb. brown sugar, ½ lb. citron. 2 lbs. each of hickory and walnuts chopped fine, ½ nutmeg, cinnamon and cloves to taste, 5 eggs, ½ cup brandy. 2 tablespoonfuls of baking soda.

A. ECKEBRECHT.

SWEET STRAWBERRY CAKE. — Three eggs, one cupful of sugar, two of flour, one tablespoonful of butter, a heaping teaspoonful of baking powder. Beat the butter and sugar together and add the eggs well beaten. Stir in the flour and baking powder well sifted together. Bake in deep tin plates; this quantity will fill four plates. With three pints of strawberries mix a cup of sugar, mash them a little. Spread fruit between layers. The top may be covered with a meringue of the white of an egg and a tablespoonful of powdered sugar.

N. K. M.

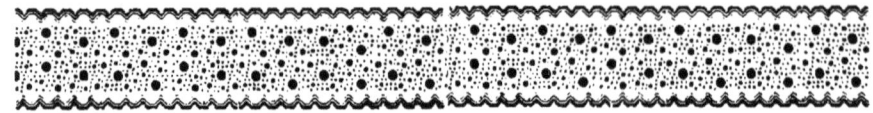

Neuberg's Express & Storage Co.,

Private Rooms for Storage

- - - if desired.

Furniture

=AND

Piano Movers

217 North Clark Street.

TELEPHONE NORTH-233.

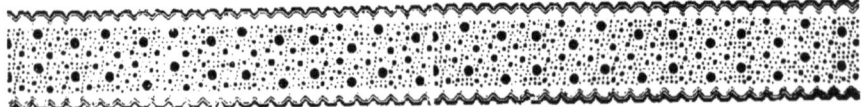

SPICE CAKE. ---- 1 cup sugar, ½ cup of butter or lard, ½ cup of milk, 3 eggs, ¼ nutmeg, ½ teaspoonful cinnamon, ½ teaspoonful cloves, 1 teaspoonful allspice.

Emma C. Braun.

SPONGE CAKE. ---- No. 1: 1 cup flour, 1 cup sugar, 3 well beaten eggs, 1½ tablespoonfuls of milk, 1 heaping teaspoonful of baking powder. Flavor with vanilla.

Lanie Braun.

MOLASSES CAKE. ---- 1 cup molasses, ½ cup sugar, 2 eggs, ⅔ cup of ice water, ½ cup butter, 2 teaspoonfuls of soda, 3½ cups of flour, and 1 cup raisins; cinnamon, allspice, ginger and cloves to taste. The soda must be put in the water, and then the part that dissolves goes into the cake, but the sediment in the bottom of the cup is not to be poured into the mixture. The raisins are to be floured; the batter is made about the same consistency as ordinary cake batter.

Ida Schmidt.

SPICE CAKE. — 1 egg, 1 cup sour milk, ½ cup butter, 1 cup raisins, 1 teaspoonful baking soda, 1 teaspoonful baking powder, 1 teaspoonful allspice, 1 teaspoonful essence of lemon, 1½ cup flour.

Lizzie Belleisle.

TELEPHONE NORTH-164.

C. E. Crozet & Co.,

WHOLESALE AND RETAIL DEALERS IN

Wall Paper, Paints, Etc.

225 N. Clark St.

INTERIOR DECORATIONS.
... FINE PAPER HANGINGS. ...
ESTIMATES FURNISHED.

Exclusive Agents and Jobbers to the Trade

of

~≋ Birge's Wall Papers ≋~

at Factory Prices.

·HICKORY NUT LAYER CAKE. — ¾ cupful butter, 2 cups sugar, 1½ pints flour, 5 eggs, 1 teaspoonful Price's baking powder. 1 cupful milk. Rub the butter and sugar to a white light cream. add the eggs, 2 at a time, beating 5 minutes between each addition. Sift the flour with the powder, add to the butter, etc., and the milk, mix into rather thin batter and bake in jelly tins 15 minutes. Before cooling, spread clear icing and hickory nuts chopped fine between layers. For icing take 1½ cups sugar, whites of 3 eggs, mix together smooth and pour over the cake.

Emma Becker.

SPONGE CAKE. — 1 lb. sugar, 1 doz eggs, 1 lb. flour, grated peel of a lemon. Sift the sugar and break the eggs in one after the other, stir about 20 minutes, sift the flour 3 or 4 times, stir it in gradually. put in form and bake in a moderate oven about one hour.

Ida Nau.

ANGEL COCOANUT CAKE. — Two cups of powdered sugar. one of butter, three of flour. one teaspoonful baking powder, whites of eight eggs, half a cup of milk. Flavor with vanilla. Bake in jelly pans. Spread the top of each with thick icing, let dry and sprinkle thickly with cocoanut. When the cake is as large as desired. ice all over and sprinkle with the cocoanut.

Olive E. Webster.

COFFEE CAKE. — 1 cup brown sugar, 1 cup of butter, 1 cup of strained coffee, 1 cup of molasses, 3 eggs well beaten, 1 lb. raisins, 4 cups of flour and two scant teaspoonfuls of saleratus.

H. K.

L. C. TEWES & CO.

Telephone North-191.

Silver · Lake · Ice,

Families promptly supplied.

297 ILLINOIS STREET.

L. WESEMANN,

COTTAGE ∴ HILL ∴ DAIRY,

135 MICHIGAN STREET.

Hotels and Restaurants supplied.

CREAM CAKE. ---- Four eggs, whites and yolks beaten separately, two teacups of sugar, one cup of sweet cream, two heaping cupfuls of flour, one teaspoonful of soda; mix two teaspoonfuls of cream of tartar in the flour before sifting. Add the whites the last thing before the flour, and stir that in gently without beating.

Adelaide Lindow.

ORANGE CAKE. — 2 cups of sugar, ½ cup of butter, beaten to a cream, 3 eggs, yolks and whites beaten separately, 1 cup of milk, 3 teaspoonfuls baking powder, 3 cups of flour and grated rind of one and juice of half an orange. Put the juice of the other half orange in the icing.

Lizzie Fricke.

NUT CAKE. --- One tablespoonful of butter and one cup of sugar, which should be beaten together, yolks of two eggs, one cup of chopped nuts, one cup of milk, two cups of flour, two heaping teaspoonfuls of baking powder, mix together, flavor with vanilla. Frosting: Beat the whites of two eggs and one pound of pulverized sugar, and decorate with nuts.

Lizzie Schodosky.

RATTAN COFFEE CAKE. --- 1 lb. of flour, ¼ cup of sugar, ¼ lb. of butter, 5 eggs, 1 cup luke warm milk, 1 cake of yeast dissolved in portion of milk. Mix butter and sugar, add eggs one by one and then the milk, yeast and flour alternately. Work the cake well one hour. Let it rise three hours and bake one hour.

Mary Yahnke.

The Highest Type.

ST▲RCK

PHIL. A. STARCK, PRES.
M. E. STRACK,
SEC. AND TREAS.

PIANOS

Sold direct from our factory at manufacturers prices.

Eass Payments if desired.

Highest Quality of Tone.   **Responsive Action.**
Delicate Touch.   **Perfect Workmanship.**
Fine Finish.   **Great Durability.**
Fully Warranted.

The above cut shows the interior view of our Grand Upright Scale Piano, with Full Iron Plate to the top of case leaving an opening where the pins go into the wrest plank. With this improvement the tone is sweet and sympathetic and the instrument will remain in tune to a greater length of time. Bridge is made of several layers of hard Rock Maple. Wrest plank of five thicknesses of the same material crossbanded. French Repeating Action, giving prompt and elastic touch. Also many other improvements which lack of space prevents us from mentioning here. Our new catalogue will be sent upon application.

Starck & Strack Piano Co.,

Salesrooms and factory: 171 & 173 South Canal St.

CHEAP FRUIT CAKE. — ½ cup molasses, ½ cup butter, 1 cup sugar, 2 cups flour, ½ cup coffee, 1 cup raisins, 1 cup almonds (or any nuts), 1 cup currants, 2 eggs, 1 teaspoonful soda dissolved in water, 2 teaspoonfuls cinnamon, ½ of cloves, 1 of brandy or wine, ¼ lb. citron, ½ nutmeg. Bake in slow oven 1 hour.

Mrs. J. Tiedemann.

EVERYDAY CAKE. ⅔ cup of butter, ⅔ cup milk, 1½ cups sugar, 2½ cups flour, 2 eggs, 1 teaspoonful vanilla, 2 teaspoonfuls Price's baking powder.

Emma Hild.

COFFEE CAKE. — Two cups of brown sugar, 1 cup new molasses, 1 cup butter, 1 cup strong coffee, 3 eggs, 1 heaping teaspoonful saleratus, 1 tablespoonful each of cinnamon, cloves and nutmeg, 1½ lb. of fruit and 5 cups of flour.

Mrs. Leupold.

FRENCH CREAM CAKE. One cup sugar and 3 eggs well beaten together, one and a half cups of flour, 2 teaspoonfuls of baking powder, well mixed, 3 tablespoons of water. Custard: Take nearly a pint of milk, heat and when nearly boiling add two small tablespoons corn starch, wet with a little cold milk, two beaten eggs, with one-half cup of sugar; cook and stir all the time until it thickens enough to drop from a spoon without running. Remove from the stove and add one-half cup of melted butter. When a little cool add 2 teaspoons of vanilla. Spread between layers while warm.

Clara Uchtmann.

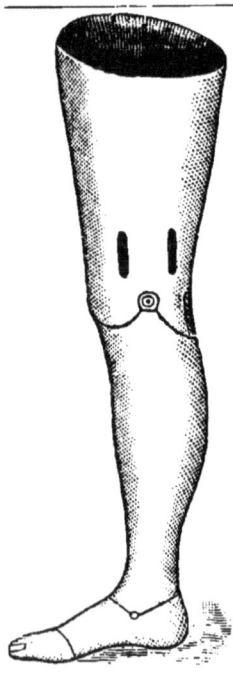

—88—

CAKE. — Eight eggs, ten ounces of sugar, half a pound of flour, the juice and rind of one lemon. Separate the eggs, beat the yolks, sugar and lemon until thick and light, whisk the whites until dry, which add with the flour, half of each at a time, mix all together, but avoid beating. Butter your pan well and bake in a moderate oven.

P. S.—Cut cake in half and spread whipped cream between.

Mrs. P. Westermann, Niobrara, Neb.

FRIED CAKES. — 1 cup of sugar, ½ cup of butter, 3 eggs; stir to a cream and add 1 cup of sweet milk, 2 teaspoons baking powder, 1 of vanilla, use enough flour to thicken, roll soft and fry in hot lard.

Minnie Hessemer.

DELICATE CAKE. - 2 cups sugar, ½ cup butter, 1 cup milk, 2 cups flour, half cup corn-starch, 1 heaping teaspoonful baking powder, whites of 4 eggs beaten, flavor with vanilla. Frosting: Boil one-half cups of sugar, half cup water, until it strings, remove from fire, pour into whites of two eggs, beaten well, add one square of grated chocolate. Stir thoroughly until cold. Apply when cake is cold. Bake in large shallow pan.

Annie Spoerer.

HICKORY NUT CAKE. — 1 cup of chopped nuts, 1½ cups sugar, half cup butter, 2 cups flour, ¾ cup milk, 2 teaspoons baking powder, whites of four eggs, well beaten.

Emma Heppe.

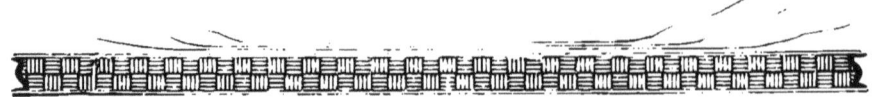

Scholl's Studio,

547 South Halsted Street,

Near 14th Street.

We recommend everybody to go to him for

BEAUTIFUL

and all kinds of **Photographs, Pictures.**

Flowers, Bouquet and Laces free.

CARAMEL CAKE. — 2 cups sugar, half cup butter, 1 cup milk, two and a half cups flour, 2 teaspoonfuls of baking powder, whites of four eggs, bake in layers. Caramel: 1 lb. C. sugar, ¾ cup milk or cream, butter size of an egg, boil 10 minutes, flavor with vanilla.

Miss Agnes Weinberger.

FIG CAKE. — 1½ cups sugar, ½ cup butter, 2½ cups flour, ¼ cup sweet milk, the whites of 6 eggs beaten stiff, 2 teaspoonfuls baking powder. For filling: 1 lb. of figs chopped, 1 cup of sugar, ½ cup of water, put on the stove and boil 15 minutes, spread between the layers.

Mary Pretzel.

CREAM LAYER CAKE. — 1 cup of sugar, 1 egg, a tablespoon of butter, 1 cup sweet milk, 2 teaspoonfuls of baking powder, 2 cups of flour, flavor with vanilla. Cream: 1½ cups of milk, ½ cup sugar, 1 egg, 2 teaspoons of corn starch, a little milk to dissolve it, mix egg and corn starch and flavor with vanilla.

H. Lang.

MINNEHAHA CAKE. — White part: Whites of 3 eggs, ¾ cup sugar, ⅓ cup butter, 6 tablespoonfuls sweet milk, 1 teaspoon baking powder, ½ cup flour, ½ cup corn starch, flavor with lemon. Red part: 2 eggs, ¼ cup butter, ¾ cup sugar, 6 tablespoons of sweet milk, 1 teaspoon of baking powder, 1 cup of flour, 1 teaspoon of fruit-coloring, flavor with vanilla. Yellow part: Yolks of 3 eggs, ¼ cup of butter, ¾ cup of sugar, 6 tablespoonfuls milk, 1 cup flour, 1 teaspoonful baking powder, flavor with vanilla. Icing: 12 tablespoonfuls powdered sugar, whites of 3 eggs beaten; place between the layers with hickory nuts or chopped raisins.

Alwine Spoerer.

GEO. W. HURST,

DEALER IN

⇒Fresh and Salt Meats, Poultry, Game,⇐

Oysters, Fish, Vegetables, Fruits, Etc.

246 N. STATE STREET.

Goods delivered free of charge.

H. C. MILLER,

Dealer in

Pure Milk & Cream,

198 ONTARIO STREET.

Springerle. — Man rührt 1 Pfund fein gesiebten Zucker mit 4 frischen Eiern eine Stunde lang, arbeitet 1 Pfund feines Mehl darunter, nimmt dann etwas von dem Teig auf ein Backbrett, rollt es eines Messerrückens dick aus, gibt dem Springerle ihre Form, läßt sie ein paar Stunden oder über Nacht liegen, bäckt sie in einem Blech, das man mit Butter gestrichen und mit Anis bestreut hat, in einem nicht sehr heißen Ofen mehr weiß als braun.

Rosina Munz.

Mürbe Teig. — 1 Pfund Mehl, 4 Eier, ½ Pfund Butter, 12 Unzen Zucker, 1 Theelöffel hartshorn salt, geknetet, ausgerollt und mit Formen ausgestochen.

Christine Rentz.

Gugelhopf. — 3 Tassen Mehl, 1 Tasse Milch, ⅜ Tasse Zucker, ½ Pfund Butter, 7 Eier, für 2c Hefe, ½ Theelöffel Salz, ¼ Citronenschale abgerieben. Die Hälfte des Mehls wird mit der Hefe und Milch zum Vorteig angerührt. Die Butter wird in eine Schüssel gethan und zu Schaum gerührt, dann werden abwechselnd Eier und Mehl hinzugerührt, wie auch Zucker, Citrone und Salz, und zuletzt der Vorteig tüchtig mit dem Löffel geschlagen. Man füllt in eine mit Butter gestrichene Form und setzt dann weg zum Gehen. In einem mäßigheißen Ofen eine Stunde zu backen.

Emma Rau.

Nürnberger Lebkuchen. — Man läßt eine Gall. Syrup aufkochen, gießt über 12 Pfund gesiebtes Mehl, läßt es etwas abkühlen und thut dazu: 1 Pfund zerstoßene Mandeln, ¼ Pfund gestoßenes Citronat, ¼ Pfund ditto Lemonat. 1 Tasse Butter, für 25 Cent Catanum, etwas mace Muskatnuß, 4 Eßlöffel Nelken, 4 Eßlöffel Zimmt, ¼ Pf. potash in Brandy aufgelöst.

Margaretha Kießling.

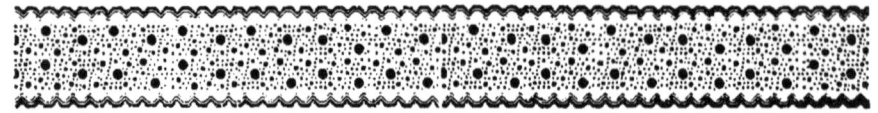

The Lincoln National Bank,

North Clark & Michigan Sts.

STRONG,

CONVENIENT,

ACCOMMODATING.

Special Attention to North Side Accounts.

DR, V. C. PRICE, PRESIDENT.

EDWARD HAMMETT, CASHIER.

J. R. CLARKE, ASS'T. CASHIER.

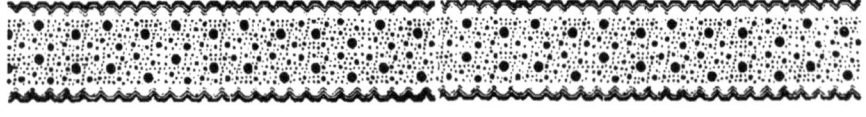

Fruit Cake. — 1 Pfund Mehl, 1 Pfund Zucker, ¾ Pfund Butter, 2 Pfund Corinthen, 2 Pfund Rosinen, 1 Pfund Citronat, ¼ Unze Muskatblüthe, 1 Weinglas Branntwein, ebensoviel Wein, 8 Eier. Man rührt Eier, Zucker und Butter tüchtig zusammen, gibt Mehl zu, dann Wein und Branntwein, Gewürz und schließlich das Uebrige. 2 Stunden langsam backen.

Lizzie Kolb.

———

Schnee=Waffeln. — Man rührt ¼ Pfund Butter zu Sahne und nach und nach 10 Eidotter, eine Prise Salz, 4 oz. Zucker, 1 abge= riebene Citronenschale und 20 oz. Mehl darunter. Die Masse wird mit circa ¼ Qt. süßer Sahne verdünnt. Zuletzt zieht man den sehr steifgeschlagenen Schnee von den 10 Eidottern darunter und bäckt schnell.

Frau P. Ohle.

———

Recept für Buttergebackenes. — ¾ Pfund Butter, 1 Pfund Zucker, 6 Eier, etwas Zimmt, Anis, Citrone, dann wenn man will, etwas Citronat und Orangenat. Die Butter zuerst gerührt, dann Zucker, Eier u. s. w., zuletzt soviel Mehl als nöthig zum Ausarbeiten und dann etwas flüchtig Salz (zum Treiben.) Man welgt den Teig auf einem Brette aus und sticht mit kleinen Formen aus. Man läßt in mit Butter und Mehl bestrichenem Blech bei mäßiger Hitze backen, bis sie gelblich braun sind.

Frau Wm. Vollmer.
Hermosa, Jlls.

———

Sand Torte. — ¾ Pf. Zucker, ¾ Pf. Mehl, 9 oz. Butter, 1 Pt. Eigelb, ½ Pt. Eiweiß zu Schnee; Zucker und Eigelb gut gerührt, dann Schnee und Mehl einmeliert und zuletzt die Butter flüßig warm eingerührt.

Wm. Nusser.

—96—

Brob = Torte. — ½ Pfund Zucker, ¼ Pfund gestoßene Man=
deln, ¼ Pfund gestoßenes gesiebtes Schwarzbrot, ½ oz. Citronat, ¼
oz. Citronenschale, Nelken und Zimmt nach Gutdünken und 11 Eier.
Der Zucker wird mit den Eidottern ¾ Stunde gerührt, dann schlägt man
das Weiße der Eier zu Schnee, mischt Alles zusammen, und zwar ab=
wechselnd Schnee und von der anderen Masse. Man füllt in die Form
und bäckt in guter Hitze.

Frau C. M. Weinberger,

Brob = Torte. — 1½ Tasse feiner Zucker, ¼ Pfund gehackte
Mandeln, 11 Eier, von 6 das Weiße zu Schnee geschlagen, 2 Tassen
getrocknetes, gestoßenes, gesiebtes Weißbrod, _ Theelöffel Zimmt, eine
Messerspitze Nelken, 3 oz. feingehacktes Citronat, etwas abgeriebene
Citronen= und Orangenschale und eine Messerspitze Potasche. Das Ci=
tronat wird mit Zucker, Mandeln und Eiern eine halbe Stunde gerührt,
nachher das Andere dazugethan, die Form geschmiert mit Weckenmehl o.
auch geriebenem Zwieback bestreut, gefüllt, in den Ofen gestellt und eine
Stunde langsam gebacken. Man bestreiche die Torte mit einem Choco=
laden=Guß.

Frau Pauline Müller.

Brob = Torte. — 15 Eier, ¼ Pfund Zucker, ½ Tasse geriebenes
und gesiebtes Schwarzbrod, 1 Tasse geriebene süße Chocolade, 3 oz. ge=
hacktes Citronat, 3 oz. gehackte Mandeln, 1 Glas Rothwein, ¼ Glas
Arrac, Gewürz nach Belieben. Eidotter, Zucker, Mandeln, Citronat
werden eine halbe Stunde gerührt, dann das Brod, mit dem Wein an=
gefeuchtet dazugethan, dann die Chocolade, Gewürz und Arrac, und zu=
letzt der Eiweiß=Schaum dazugerührt. Gleich in einen mittelmäßig hei=
ßen Ofen bringen und 1 Stunde backen.

Lily Gloeckler.

M. KECK,

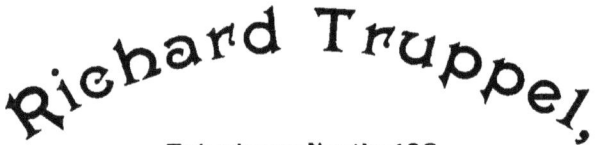

—DEALER IN—

Hardware, Stoves,

and Tinware,

645 LINCOLN AVE.

All House Furnishing Goods.

Builders' Hardware a Specialty. All kinds of Tin and Sheet-iron
work to order.

Richard Truppel,

Telephone North-426.

Apotheker,

96 WELLS STR., ECKE INDIANA

Brod Torte mit Mandeln. — 18 Eidotter, 1 Pfund Zucker, 6 oz. gehackte Mandeln, 1 Eßlöffel gestoßenen Zimmt, 1 oz. fein geschnittenes Citronat, ½ geriebene Citronenschale und 6 oz. getrocknetes und fein gestoßenes Roggenbrod benetzt mit einem Glas Rothwein. Diese Masse rühre gut zusammen, füge das zu Schnee geschlagene Eiweiß hinzu, fülle in eine mit Butter bestrichene Pfanne und backe 1 Stunde in mäßig heißem Ofen.

Emma H. Merki.

Blitzkuchen. — ½ Tasse Butter, 1 Tasse Zucker, etwas geriebene Citronenschale, rühre zu Schaum, füge hinzu 2 Tassen Mehl, 1 Theelöffel Backpulver und ein wenig Milch. Streiche dünn in eine mit Butter geriebne Pfanne, streue Zimmt, Zucker, gehackte Mandeln darauf, backe in sehr heißem Ofen und schneide heiß.

Emma H. Merki.

ECONOMICAL CAKE. — One cup sugar, ½ cup butter, whites of 3 eggs, ½ cup sweet milk, 2 cups flour, 1 heaping teaspoonful Dr. Price's baking powder. Bake in two layers. Frosting: Yolks of 3 eggs, 1 cup pulverized sugar, 1 teaspoonful vanilla; beat 20 minutes and spread between the layers and on the top.

Clara Wiese.

ALMOND LAYER CAKE. — 1 cup sugar, ½ cup butter, 5 eggs, 1¾ cups flour, 1½ teaspoonfuls baking powder, flavor with lemon or vanilla; this makes 4 layers. Filling: ¼ lb. sweet almonds chopped fine, 1 pint cream, boil together, a little sugar to sweeten it, then thicken with cornstarch dissolved in water, stir in the yellow of an egg and flavor with vanilla. Frosting: Take powdered sugar and water enough to make a paste and flavor with vanilla.

Emilie Wehland.

—100—

ICING CAKE. — 2 cups sugar, ¾ cup butter, 1 cup of milk, 3 cups flour, whites of 5 eggs, 3 teaspoons of baking powder. Bake in 3 layers. Icing: 2 cups sugar, half cup water. Boil sugar and water until thick and waxy. Then pour over the whites of two well beaten eggs, beating all the time, and add juice of one lemon.

Mrs. P. W. Neudoerfer.

ICE-CREAM CAKE. — Make good sponge cake, bake ½ in. thick in jelly tins and let it get perfectly cold. Icing: 1 pint thickened sweet cream beaten until it looks like ice-cream, make it very sweet and flavor with vanilla. Blanch and chop 1 lb. almonds, stir into cream and spread between layers.

Lillie Busch.

SILVER CAKE. — 1½ cups of sugar, ½ cup of butter, 1 cup of sweet milk, 2 teaspoonfuls Price's baking powder, 3 cups of flour, whites of 6 eggs beaten to a stiff froth, flavor with bitter almonds.

Mrs. Haman.

WINE CAKE. — One pt. of sweet milk, 3 eggs well beaten with a teaspoonful of salt. Flour enough to make batter similar to pan cakes. Have hot lard and try as you would a fry cake. Then take a spoonful of butter and let your hand shake as you drop it in the lard. Serve warm with wine and sugar or sweet cream.

Emma Schick.

J. G. OTTMANN,

Carpenter and Contractor,

422 Cleveland Avenue.

Alterations and Repairing promptly attended to.

Telephone Main-4922.

The Chicago Mirror & Art Glass Co.

Manufacturers of

French Looking Glass Plates,

Cut, Embossed Beveled and Ornamental Glass.

54 to 60 North
CLINTON STREET.

Old Mirrors Re-silvered.

John H. Haake, Secretary.

BRIDE CAKE. — 1½ lbs. butter, 1¾ lbs. sugar, half of which is to be Orleans sugar, 4 lbs. seeded raisins chopped, 5 lbs. of English currants, 2 lbs. sifted flour, 2 nutmegs, 20 eggs well beaten, 2 lbs. citron cut fine and mace to taste; 1 gill to ½ pt. of alcohol in which a dozen to 15 drops of oil of lemon have been put.

Mary Schnell.

———

BOSTON CAKE. — 2 ¼ lbs. flour, 1¾ lbs. sugar, 1¼ lbs. butter, 3 lbs. raisins, 3 nutmegs, 8 eggs, ½ pt. brandy, ⅓ pt. milk and 3 teaspoonfuls of baking powder.

Minnie Jacobs.

———

MANDEL TORTE. — 9 eggs, 1 lb. powdered sugar, ½ lb. almonds, 3 zwieback or 1 cup grated bread, rind of 1 lemon, teaspoon baking powder. Beat yolks and sugar ½ hour, then add bread and almonds, lastly whites beaten to stiff froth. Bake 1 hr. slowly.

H. Lupsch.

Pies.

———

COCOANUT PIE. — ½ cocoanut, grated, yolks of 4 eggs, 4 tablespoonfuls sugar, add milk as for custard pie. Frosted.

Emily Sonnenschein.

———

Michener's  Celebrated

'Banana Brand'

Ham

and

Bacon.

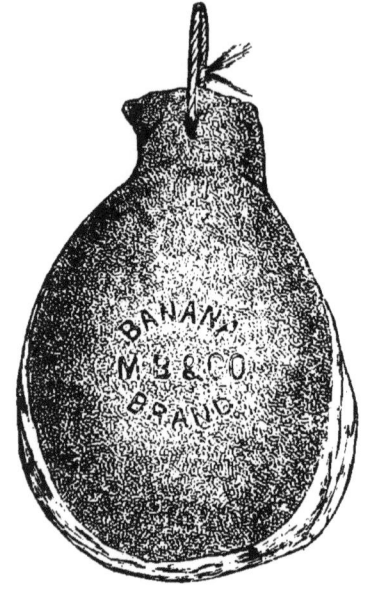

Philadelphia.   **Chicago.**

SOLD BY

GEO. A. ARNOLD,

Lakeside Market,

Choice Meats, Poultry, Game, Vegetables, Etc.

735 WELLS STREET.

Orders taken and personally attended to,

APPLE PIE. — Make a thick sliced apple pie, seasoning with cinnamon or nutmeg and a little butter, no sugar. Make a small opening in the center of the upper crust. Bake until thoroughly done. Cook 1 cup or 1½ cups of sugar, according to sourness of apples, till it becomes a syrup, adding water as necessary lest it be too thick. When the pie is done but still hot, pour the syrup carefully through the opening in the crust.

Ida Koch, Toledo, O.

ORANGE PIE. — 3 eggs, ¾ cup white sugar, 2 tablespoons butter, juice and grated rind of 1 orange, juice and grated rind of ½ lemon, nutmeg to taste. Beat butter and sugar together well, then beat in the yolks of the eggs, add the lemon and orange, put into pastry without top crust and bake. When done spread over them the whites of the eggs beaten stiff with powdered sugar and return to the oven for a few minutes to brown.

Annie Schnell.

CHEESE PIE. — Paste: 1 cup of butter, 2 eggs, 1 teaspoonful whisky or white wine, a good pinch of salt and a cup of good milk. Put one-half the butter into a deep bowl and add the other ingredients, add enough flour gradually to make a firm paste, stirring all the time. Place on a well floured board, roll about ½ in. thick, then take the other half of the butter and spread over the paste, fold sides of the same squarely toward the center, but be careful always to fold the same way, roll out and fold again. repeat this 4 or 5 times. Let stand in cold place at least 1 hr. (over night is better). When using, handle as little as possible; Cheese: ½ lb. good Swiss cheese grated into deep bowl, add 3 well-beaten eggs and 1 cup of milk (not boiled), mix to thickness of a custard. Fill small pie tins, lined with paste, then put a few small pieces of butter on each and bake in a quick oven about 10 minutes. ·

Mrs. Hahl.

MARKS BROS.,

FASHIONABLE TAILORS, ...

359 E. DIVISION ST.

TELEPHONE NORTH-339.

Molter & Kretschmer,

Plumbers and Gas Fitters,

Manufactuers of and Dealers in

⇥ GAS FIXTURES, ⇤

426 E. Division Street.

Sanitary Work a Specialty.

—106—

LEMON PIE. — 2 eggs, 1 cup sugar, 1 cup sweet cream, 2 tablespoons melted butter, 2 tablespoons of flour or a level tablespoon of cornstarch, the juice and grated rind of 1 lemon. This makes 1 pie.

Marion Carr.

————

LEMON PIE. — 1 cup sugar, 1 cup water, 2 eggs, 1 lemon, grated rind and juice, 3 teaspoons cornstarch. Frosted.

Mrs. E. K.

————

LEMON PIE. —— Grated rind and juice of 1 good lemon, cup of sugar and butter size of egg beaten well together, add 1 tablespoonful of cornstarch, enough cold water to make it smooth, then stir this into a cupful of boiling water in a sauce-pan; as soon as it begins to boil pour it into the butter and sugar, stir in the lemon-juice and rind and when cold stir in the beaten yolks of 2 eggs. Pour this into crust and bake like custard. Beat the whites of 2 eggs to a stiff froth with a tablespoonful of powdered sugar, pour on pie and brown slightly.

Josie Salzer.

————

LEMON PIE. —— Slice 2 lemons as thin as possible, put them in a dish, and pour over 1½ teacups of sugar. Cut the pulpy parts so as to have the juice escape freely, add 1½ teacups of water and 2 eggs well beaten. Bake between 2 crusts. This will make 2 pies.

Annie Petersen.

William Nusser,

FANCY BAKERY AND CAFE,

131 North Clark Street.

Orders promptly attended to.

Berry & Walker,

Carpenters and Builders,

519 Melrose Street,

Jas, Bodmer,

Mason and Contractor,

432 E. Division Street.

Residence, 1483 Roscoe St.

MINCE MEAT. ---- Boil 4 lbs. of good beef and chop fine, 8 lbs. of apples (greenings) chopped, 2 lbs. of beef suet chopped, 2 lbs. of stoned raisins, 2 lbs. of currants, 1 lb. citron, 2 nutmegs, 1 qt. syrup, 5 teaspoonfuls of cloves, 5 of cinnamon, salt to taste, 2 lbs. brown sugar, 2 lemons, sweet cider enough to moisten, 1 pt. of brandy. After all is chopped mix well and boil together, put away in stone jar.

Mrs. Amelia Bross.

MINCE MEAT. — Boil nice meat quite tender, using a small quantity of water. When done remove the bones and gristle and keep the liquor. When the meat is cold, chop it fine; if lean, add chopped suet or butter, add a little salt. Add half the quantity of apples, 1 cup of syrup, 2 of brown sugar. Place all with the beef liquor in a porcelain kettle, add half a pound of chopped raisins and $\frac{1}{2}$ pt. cider. When ready for making pies, add nutmeg, cinnamon, cloves and allspice to taste, and a cup of wincor brandy if desired.

Kate Hoffmann.

MINCE MEAT. ---- 1¾ lbs. lean beef, 1 lb. raisins, 1½ lbs. currants, 1 lb. beef suet, 1 lb. sugar, 1 oz. citron, 1 of lemon peel, 1 oz. orange peel, ½ nutmeg, 1 doz. apples, rind of 1 lemon, juice of ½ lemon, ¼ pint brandy. Mix these ingredients well together, adding brandy last. Press the whole into a jar, exclude the air, and it is ready for use in two weeks.

Clara Veesenmeyer.

—110—

Kartoffel Pubbing. — 12 oz. geriebene Kartoffeln, 4 Eier, 6 oz. Butter, 5 oz. Zucker, Saft und Schale einer Citrone, das Weiße der Eier zu Schnee, 1½ Stunde kochen. Servirt mit Obst.

Christine Rentz.

Schnee = Pubbing. — ½ Päckchen Gelatine mit 1 Tasse kalt Wasser begossen, dazu 1½ Tasse Zucker. Wenn aufgelöst giebt man eine Tasse kochendes Wasser dazu, Saft einer Citrone, das Weiße von 4 Eiern zu Schnee. Man rührt alles zusammen bis es leicht und schaumig ist oder bis Gelatine sich nicht mehr an den Boden setzt. Man gibt dies auf ein Glas Geschirr nebst einem Custard gemacht von 1 Pt. Milch, den Dottern von 4 Eiern, 4 Eßlöffel Zucker und geriebener Schale einer Citrone. Gekocht.

Frau John Baur.

Kartoffel = Pubbing. — 2½ Pfund gekochte geriebene Kartoffeln, ¼ Pfund geriebenes altes Weißbrod, knapp ½ Pfund Butter, reichlich ½ Pfund Zucker, 2 Eßlöffel gestoßene bittere und süße Mandeln, 9 Eier, 1 abgeriebene Citrone und den Saft derselben. Die Butter wird zu Sahne gerührt, dann werden Zucker, Mandeln, Citrone und nach und nach die Eidotter wie auch die geriebenen Kartoffeln hinzu gerührt. Nachdem die Masse mit dem geriebenen Weißbrot gut durchgemengt ist, kommt zuletzt noch der feste Schaum der Eier dazu. Dann füllt man alles in eine gut ausgestrichene und ausgestreute geschlossene Form und läßt den Pubbing 2 Stunden kochen. Man gibt gekochtes Obst oder eine Fruchtsauce dazu.

Frau Lucie Rahtjen.

Chocolade = Pudding. — ¼ Pfund Butter, ½ Pfund ge=
siebten Zucker, 12 Eier, ¼ Pfund geriebene oder fein gestoßene Man=
deln, 6¼ oz. geriebene und durchgesiebte Chocolade, et oas mit Zucker
fein gestoßene Vanille oder Zimmt. Die Butter wird zu Sahne gerie=
ben, nach und nach werden Zucker, Eidotter, Mandeln, Chocolade und
Vanille hinzugefügt, ¼ Stunde stark gerührt, das zu Schaum geschlagene
Eiweiß leicht durchgemischt und der Pudding 1 Stunde bei mittelmäßiger
Hitze gebacken. Will man denselben kalt zu geben, so wird er zwei
Stunden gekocht und Vanillensauce dazu gegeben.

Anna Moese.

———

Gebackenes Aepfelcompott mit Mandelguß. —
Es wird ein fein zubereitetes dickes Apfelmus gekocht, zu einer Kompot=
tiere zwei zu Schaum geschlagene Eiweiß heiß durchgerührt und solches
glatt angerichtet. Dann wird eine Handvoll geriebene Mandeln mit
Zucker, Zimmt, etwas Citronensaft und dem Schaum von 2 bis 3 Eiern
gelb gebacken und, wenn's beliebt, kalt mit Gelee verziert.

E. Haeske.

———

Weintrauben = Pudding. — (Sehr zu empfehlen.) ¼
Pfund Butter, 8 Eier, ¼ Pfund fein gestoßene Mandeln, ½ Pf. Pul=
verzucker, Zimmt nach Belieben, ebenso Citronenschale, ¼ Pfund abge=
schältes Weißbrod, ein Suppenteller abgepflückte Trauben. Man rührt
die Butter zu Sahne, gibt Eidotter, Zucker, Gewürz und das Weißbrot
dazu. Man mischt, nachdem die Masse stark gerührt ist, die Beeren
nebst dem Eiweißschaum durch.

E. Haeske.

———

SPANISH CREAM. —— 1 pt. milk, ½ box gelatine, boil together. Yolks of 3 eggs, sugar to taste, stir this in boiling milk,
add the whites, well beaten, flavor with vanilla, then turn in a
form. Set on ice.

Anna Sonnenschein.

The G. H. A. Thomas Co.

Long Leaf Yellow Pine,

MILLS AT SPRINGFIELD, LA.

Chicago Office, 92 Washington Street.

Dr. John W. Maier,

✠✠✠ Dentist,

1206 E. Baltimore Street,

Baltimore, Md.

Snow. —— Half package of gelatine, 3 eggs, 2 cups sugar, juice of 2 lemons. Soak gelatine 1 hour in a cup of cold water, add 1 pint of boiling water and stir until dissolved. Beat the whites of the eggs to a stiff froth. When gelatine is quite cold, mix all together and beat 40 minutes or until stiff. Pour into a mold or glasses previously wet with cold water and put in a cool place. Make a custard of 1½ pints of milk, yolks of the eggs and ¼ cup of sugar, flavor with vanilla. When the snow is poured out of the mold, pour the custard around the base.

Minnie Jacobs.

Fig Pudding. —— 1 lb. figs, 1 lb. raisins, 2 lbs. currants, ½ lb. almonds, chopped fine, 1 lb. of bread crumbs, 6 eggs, a little water, suet the size of a goose-egg (chopped fine). Boil in custard kettle 4 hours.

Martha John, Trenton, Ill.

Gelatine Pudding. —— 1 pint milk, ½ package gelatine, 3 eggs, 1 cup sugar and 1 teaspoonful vanilla. Put milk on the stove and let it get hot, add your sugar, then soak gelatine in enough hot water to dissolve it; strain this into the milk and add the beaten yolks of the eggs and stir. Do not let it boil or it may curdle, just keep it hot. Now stir in the whites of the eggs beaten to a stiff froth and take off the stove and flavor. While hot, pour into a mold and set away to cool. This makes an excellent gelatine pudding to be eaten with plain cream.

Tillie Fischbeck.

English Christmas Plum Pudding. —— 1 lb. stoned raisins and currants, 1 lb. suet, finely chopped, ¼ lb. bread crumbs or flour, 3 oz. sugar, 1½ oz. grated lemon peel, blade of mace, half a nutmeg, teaspoon ginger, ½ doz. eggs well beaten. Mix well, put in cloth, tie firmly, allowing room to swell. Boil not less than 2 hrs. in boiling water.

Katie Schnell.

—116—

ENGLISH PLUM PUDDING. — 1 cup chopped suet, 1 cup milk, 1 cup raisins, 1 cup currants, 1½ cups molasses, ⅓ cup sugar, 3 cups flour, 2 teaspoons cream tartar, 1 teaspoon baking soda, 1 teaspoon salt, 1 teaspoon ginger, 1 teaspoon cinnamon. Nutmeg to taste, steam 3 hours and serve with vanilla sauce.

Lizzie Heppe.

———

VIENNESE PUDDING. — 1 pt. cream, 2 tablespoonfuls of flour, the yolks of 5 eggs, 2 oz. almonds lightly chopped, the crumbs of a French roll grated, ¼ lb. fresh butter, 3 oz. sugar, the rind of two small lemons grated. Mix the cream and flour lightly together, then add the yolks of the eggs, almonds, grated roll and lemon rind and the melted butter, stir well together; pour into a buttered mold and bake 20 minutes.

Sophie Mahr.

———

PRUNE PUDDING. — Boil ½ lb. prunes; when done, dry between two towels and chop fine. The beaten whites of 4 eggs, 3 tablespoonfuls of powdered sugar, add the prunes and 2 teaspoons of vanilla, beat all lightly together, put in a deep dish and bake in a moderate oven 15 minutes. When cold, serve with cream.

Mrs. Lena Nissen.

———

PEACH PUDDING. — One can or 12 large peaches, 2 cups of sugar, 1 pint of water and whites of 3 eggs; break peaches and stir all together, freeze the whole into form and beat the eggs to a froth.

Mrs. Eva Becker.

PRUNE PUDDING. ---- Put 1 lb. prunes in a porcelain kettle, with sufficient water to prevent burning; cover the kettle and cook slowly until the prunes are very tender. Sweeten to taste and stand aside to cool. When cold, remove stones and beat with beater until reduced to a smooth pulp. Beat whites of 3 eggs to a stiff froth, add to prunes, beat until thoroughly mixed. Heap in dish and stand away to get very cold. Make a custard from a pint of milk, 2 tablespoonfuls of sugar and yolks of 3 eggs, thicken very slightly with cornstarch and when cold pour over the pudding. This is delicious if made from fine prunes.

Mamie Gross.

LEMON SPONGE. --- Lemon sponge is made from the juice of 4 lemons, 4 eggs, a cupful of sugar, half a package of gelatine and 1 pint of water Strain lemon juice on sugar. Beat the yolks of the eggs and mix with the remainder of the water, having used a half cupful of the pint in which to soak the gelatine. Add the sugar and lemon to this and cook until it begins to thicken, when add the gelatine. Strain this into a basin, which place in a pan of water to cool. Beat with a whisk until it has cooled but not hardened; now add the whites of the eggs until it begins to thicken, turn into a mold and set to harden. The sponge hardens very rapidly when it commences to cool, so have your molds ready. Serve with powdered sugar and cream.

Carrie Birk.

ALMOND PUDDING. ---- Four tablespoonfuls cornstarch, 1 qt. milk, 1 doz. almonds blanched and powdered, one half teaspoonful almond extract. Boil the milk, add the cornstarch, then the almonds. Mold and turn out on a platter. Make frosting of the whites of 6 eggs and 3 tablespoonfuls of powdered sugar, spread over the top and set in the oven until light brown.

Ella Eder.

SPANISH CREAM PUDDING. — Take one quart of milk and three parts of a package of gelatine, and dissolve the gelatine in the milk. When it boils, add the yolks of five eggs, well beaten, with five tablespoonfuls of sugar; let it boil about 10 minutes until it curdles. Then take the whites of the eggs, beat them to a stiff froth, put it in a large dish and pour boiling cream over, stir well and flavor with vanilla. Pour into a mold and set on ice until stiff. Serve with whipped cream. Must be made the day before used.

Mrs. A. Sturm.

ORANGE FLOAT. — To make orange float, take 1 quart of water, the juice and pulp of 2 lemons, 1 cupful of sugar. When boiling hot add 4 tablespoonfuls of cornstarch. Let it boil 15 minutes, stirring all the time. When cold, pour it over 4 or 5 oranges that have been sliced into a glass dish and over the top spread the beaten whites of 3 eggs, sweetened and flavored with vanilla.

L. Meyers.

BREAD PUDDING. — One pint of nice bread crumbs, 1 quart of milk, 1 cup of sugar, yolks of 4 eggs well beaten, grated rind of 1 lemon and piece of butter size of an egg. Bake until well done. Then beat whites of 4 eggs to a stiff froth, adding a teacup of powdered sugar in which has been stirred the juice of a lemon. Spread a layer of jelly over the pudding and the frosting over this. Let brown a little. Serve with cold cream.

Mrs. C. Schmidt.

BATTER PUDDING. — Stir 1 pint of flour, 2 teaspoonfuls of baking powder and pinch of salt into milk until soft, not thin. Place in the steamer well greased teacups, put in each a small teaspoonful of the batter, then a spoonful of any kind of cooked fruit, being careful to keep out the juice. Cover with another spoonful of batter and steam 25 minutes, keeping closely covered. To be eaten with cream or any other pudding sauce. The above quantity makes five cups.

Mrs. Jos. Santa.

BIRD NEST PUDDING. — Pare and core 1 doz. large apples, put in oven with a little water until almost done; then make a custard of 4 eggs, 1 teaspoonful of corn starch, 1 pint of milk and 1 cup powdered sugar, 1 tablespoon of vanilla and bake until done. Beat the whites of eggs to a stiff froth and add 1 cup of powdered sugar. When custard and apples are done, pour this over and let it brown a light brown, fill apples with jelly and serve with cream.

Mrs. Nusser.

THE QUEEN OF PUDDING. — One pint of bread crumbs, 1 quart milk, 6 oz. sugar, butter size of an egg, yolks of 4 eggs. Flavor with lemons and bake as custard. Beat the whites of 4 eggs to a froth, mix with a cup of powdered sugar and juice of a lemon. Spread a layer of fruit jelly over the custard while hot, cover with the frosting and bake until slightly brown. To be eaten cold with cream or warm with any sauce that may be preferred.

Mrs. Naper.

APPLE TAPIOCA PUDDING. — ¾ pt. tapioca soaked 2 hours in a qt. luke warm water. Add to this 1 teaspoonful of lemon extract and 3 tablespoonfuls of granulated sugar. Pour this mixture over pared and cored apples and bake in hot oven until the apples are tender. Serve with powdered sugar and cream.

Clara Stiefel.

ICE CREAM FILLING. — Make an icing as follows: Three cups of sugar, one of water; boil to a thick clear syrup or until it begins to be brittle; pour this boiling hot over the well beaten whites of three eggs, stir the mixture very briskly and pour the sugar in slowly. Beat it when all is added until cool. Flavor with lemon or vanilla extract. This spread between any white cake layers answers for ice-cream cake.

Louise Stiefel.

A SIMPLE ORANGE PUDDING. — Put in a bowl 3 tablespoonfuls of butter and 6 tablespoonfuls of powdered sugar, and beat them to a cream. Add the yolks of 6 eggs with the grated peel of a Valencia orange. Set the bowl containing the mixture in a pan of boiling water and beat it continually with an egg beater for about six minutes, then remove the bowl to the table and beat the whites of the six eggs to a froth. Then pour them gradually and carefully into the other preparation which should be a little cooled. Use the egg, beaten about six minutes more. Butter six tin pudding cups, holding about 2 gills each. Dredge a little sugar over the inside of them. Divide the preparation equally between the six cups, set them in a tin pan of warm water reaching half way up the cups and place them in a moderately hot oven to bake for fifty minutes. Serve them turned out of the cups on a low dessert plate with this sauce. Break two raw eggs into a saucepan and a teaspoonful of flour and two tablespoonfuls of sugar. Beat the mixture thoroughly and pour over it a cup and a half of boiling milk. Stir over the fire until it boils; add a cup of good sherry and serve it with the pudding at once.

Alma Atzel.

Pickles, Jellies ꝛc.

Tomato Sauce. — 24 große Tomatos, 4 große Zwiebeln, 4 grüne Pfeffer, 3 Eßlöffel braunen Zucker, 6 Tassen Essig. Hacke Zwiebel und Pfeffer fein. Koche Alles zusammen 1½ Stunde. Schneide Tomatos, Theelöffel voll Nelken und ebensoviel Gewürz.

Frau H. Mahnken.

CHILI SAUCE. — 18 ripe tomatoes, 4 cups vinegar, 4 large peppers, 4 onions chopped fine, 3 tablespoons sugar, 2 tablespoons salt, 2 tablespoons ground cinnamon, 1 tablespoon cloves, 1 tablespoon allspice, 1 tablespoon ginger. Boil 1 hour.

Mrs. H. POTTIE.

———

CHOW CHOW. — 2 large heads of cabbage, 25 small cucumbers, 2 dozen onions, ½ dozen peppers, one-half pint grated horse-radish, 1 oz. celery seed, ¼ lb. white mustard seed. Cut vegetables small, put in salt over night, then drain them; cover with equal parts of vinegar and water for two days, drain again and put in jars. Then boil one gallon vinegar, one lb. sugar and the spices and pour over while boiling hot: repeat three times and add prepared mustard.

Mrs. B. Eckebrecht.

———

PICCALILLY. — 1 pk. of green tomatoes, 2 heads of cabbage, 2 heads of cauliflower, 6 onions, 2 sticks horse-radish, 5 cents mustard seed, 5 cents celery seed, 6 cucumbers. Chop fine, salt and let stand over night, put in a cheese cloth bag and drain. Then put in a kettle with vinegar enough to cover and add 1 and one-half lbs. of brown sugar. Boil 1 hour and put in jars.

Mrs. Julia Wolff.

———

GREEN TOMATO PICKLE. — One peck green tomatoes sliced, 6 large onions sliced, put in alternate layers in jar and sprinkle through them one cup of salt; let stand over night, drain off in the morning. Then take two quarts of water and one of vinegar and boil the tomatoes and onions in this for five minutes, then drain through a colander and put in your kettle 4 qts. vinegar, 2 lbs. of brown sugar, one-half lb. ground mustard, 2 tablespoons ground cloves and 2 tablespoons ground ginger, one-half teaspoon red pepper. Boil 15 minutes and then put in jars.

Mrs. G. Apfel.

———

PICCALILLY. — Chop small 1 peck of green tomatoes. Squeeze the juice out and place them in a crock shaking salt over them. Chop 1 peck of small green cucumbers, one large head of cabbage, 6 large peppers, one-half peck of onions, one or two heads of cauliflower, and mix in with the tomatoes. Mix in also ¼ lbs of allspice, ¼ lb. whole pepper, one oz. of cloves. Let this mixture stand for two or three hours, then rinse out with clean cold water. Boil one gallon of vinegar and 4 lbs. of sugar and one-half oz. of cloves. Throw in some of the mixture letting it scald, then strain, placing in a crock, scattering mustard seeds over it.

Mrs. Wm. Greiner.

———

FRENCH PICKLES. — 2 dozen green tomatoes, 6 large green peppers, 2 dozen cucumbers, 1 dozen onions, 6 heads german celery, 1 head cabbage; chop all fine, 1 cup salt. Let it stand over night then empty into a colander and drain. Boil one half the mixture at a time in one qt. vinegar and one qt. water, drain this as before. Put all into a jar. Take 1 gallon vinegar, put in 3 lbs brown sugar, one cup mustard seed, 3 tablespoonfuls ground mustard, 3 tablespoonfuls cinnamon, 1 of cloves, 1 of cayenne pepper, 1 of allspice, 1 of mace, 1 oz. coriander seed adding one large red pepper cut in small strips, scald all and pour the mixture in the jar hot and cover close.

Mrs. Theo. Hohenadel.

———

Tomato Spice Catsup. — 24 große Tomatoes, schäle u· schneide sie. Dann 12 große Zwiebeln, hacke dieselben und koche Beides miteinander 2 Stunden lang. Nimm ferner 8 Tassen Essig, 4 Eßlöffel Salz, 4 Eßlöffel Zucker, 4 Theelöffel feinen Ingwer, 4 Theelöffel feinen Zimmt, 4 Theelöffel feine Nelken, 3 Theelöffel allspice, 1 knappen halben Theelöffel Pfeffer. Vermenge gut und laß wieder 3—4 Stunden kochen; rühre fleißig. Fülle heiß in Glas, verschließe gut und man kann es jahrelang halten.

Etta Heinemann.

———

Allerlei.

Apfel = Creme. — 6 große gebratene Aepfel werden durch ein Sieb gerührt mit 3 Eiweiß, Zucker nach Belieben, etwas Citronensaft ¼ St. mit dem Schneeschläger geschlagen. Man füllt es in eine Glasschale und verziert es mit Apfel= oder Himbeer=Gelee. Man kann auch ein paar Löffel Gelee unter den Creme mischen.

S. Mensing.

Wein. — 15 Pfund Trauben, gieße 1 Gallone kochendes Wasser darauf, laß 3 Tage gähren. Presse aus und gieb 4 Pfund Zucker dazu. Laß 10 Tage gähren, gieße durch ein Sieb oder Tuch, fülle in Flasche und der Wein ist fertig.

Frau Maria Schwarz.

Johannisbeer (currant) Wein. — 8 Pfund Corinthen, 5 Pfund Zucker, ¼ Gallone Wasser. Man thut die Corinthen mit den Stengeln in einen Zuber und zerdrückt sie gut, fügt das Wasser hinzu, stellt es an einen kühlen Ort und rührt es gelegentlich um, etwa 3 Tage. Dann zieht man den Saft durch ein Sieb ab, zerdrückt die Masse durch ein Tuch, fügt den Zucker zu, rührt bis er aufgelöst ist und füllt es in ein Faß oder einen Krug, und stellt in einen trocknen kühlen Keller. Wenn Gährung vorüber ist, spündet man es dicht zu und läßt es den Winter über stehen. Im Frühjahre wird der Wein abgezogen, ehe die zweite Gährung eintritt. Ist diese dann vorüber so füllt man auf Flaschen.

Frau M. Mann.

CHILI SAUCE. — 22 tomatoes, 2 onions, 2 green peppers, ¼ cup sugar, 1 cup vinegar, salt to taste, boil 1 hr.

Mrs. H. M.

JELLIED APPLES. — Butter a pudding dish and fill with pared, quartered and cored tart apples, sprinkle a lot of cinnamon or any desired spice over it, pour in a teacup cold water and one of sugar. Cover closely, set in larger vessel of hot water and bake in oven 3 hrs. When cold it can be turned out in a jellied mass.

N. N.

WINE JELLY. — ½ box gelatine, ½ cup cold water, 1 pint of boiling water, juice of 1 lemon, 1 cup of sugar, 1 cup sherry wine. Soak the gelatine in cold water 15 minutes, then add the boiling water, lemon juice and wine. Stir well and sift through a fine napkin into a mold. Set on ice and serve with cream.

Mrs. A. C. Kelwig.

SPICED CURRANTS. — 1 pk. of currants (15 lbs.), boil 15 to 20 minutes, then add 6 lbs. of brown sugar, 1 qt. of vinegar, 1 tablespoonful of cinnamon, 1 of cloves and 1 of allspice. Boil all 1 hr.

Kate Simons.

WINE JELLY. — ¾ package gelatine put in a bowl with ½ pint cold water, soak ½ hour, then add one lemon cut in slices, a pinch of salt, ½ pint wine, ½ pint sugar, 1 tablespoonful of brandy, put in a porcelain kettle, and add 1 pint boiling water. Let boil 15 minutes, strain and put in mold.

Mrs. Chas. E. Rehm.

SPICED GRAPES. — 5 lbs. fruit 1 pt. vinegar, 4 lbs. sugar, 2 tablespoons cloves, 2 tablespoons cinnamon, 2 lbs. allspice, boil 1¼ hours. Remove the skins, let the pulps come to a boil, strain through a sieve. Add sugar, spice, vinegar and skins, then boil.

Mrs. C. Broughton.

BEET PRESERVES. — To 12 beets take 3 large lemons. Peel and cut the beets in long narrow strips, grate the rind of lemons and squeeze the juice. To this add ½ pint water and 1 lb. sugar. Cook the beets in this juice on a slow fire until tender.

Augusta Hahl.

QUINCE JELLY. — Rub the quinces with a cloth until perfectly smooth, cut in small pieces, pack tight in a kettle, pour on cold water until level with the fruit, boil until soft; take a flannel bag, pour in fruit and hang up to drain; occasionally press it to make the juice run more freely, taking care not to press it hard enough to expel the pulp. To a pint of juice add 1½ pints of sugar and boil 15 minutes or until it is jelly, covering at once, but not putting away until cold. Care should be taken to make the sealing perfect.

Mrs. Minna Beck.

WILD CHERRY WINE. — Wash and dry ¼ pk. of wild cherries, put them into a demijohn that is perfectly clean. On this pour 1 gal. of best cognac brandy and 2 lbs. of loaf sugar; shake well, and in one week it is fit for use. This is a good tonic for invalids and improves with age. The cherries must be fresh and good.

Mrs. A. Andresen.

Sarbellen Sauce. — Gereinigte Sarbellen werden mit Zwiebeln fein gehackt. Man läßt in einem Topfe Butter heiß werden, röstet etwas Mehl mit Zucker braun, bringt die Sarbellen hinzu, läßt es noch etwas mit dämpfen, füllt es mit Fleischbrühe auf und läßt noch ein wenig kochen. Einige Löffel voll Kalbsbraten Sauce gehört daran, wenn's recht gut werden soll.

Anna Klinke.

BLACKBERRY WINE. — Squeeze 50 lbs. blackberries, strain, and add 25 lbs. sugar. Put into a 10 gal. jug and fill with water. Keeping it full after it works out and add 3 pts. of good brandy.

Mrs. Damler.

SAUCE HOLLANDAISE. — Put a pt. of water in a saucepan, add a slice of onion, a bay leaf, and a blade of mace. Let stand about 10 minutes on the back of the stove. While this is steeping, rub together two tablespoonfuls of butter and two of flour; add this to the water and stir until smooth and thick; then strain, return the sauce to the pan, and when boiling hot add the well-beaten yolks of two eggs. Cook a moment, being careful not to have it curdle, take from fire, add a tablespoonful of lemon juice, one of chopped parsley, a teaspoonful of salt and a dash of pepper. It is then ready for use.

Clara Schmidt.

CHOCOLATE DROPS. — 1 lb. powdered sugar, ½ lb. almonds chopped fine, 1 teaspoon cloves, 2 teaspoons cinnamon, whites of 4 eggs, chocolate enough to stiffen. Stir 1 hour and bake in moderate oven.

Mrs. A. H. Grunewald.

Apfelschnitte. — Es werden schöne große Aepfel geschält, in etwas dicke Scheiben geschnitten. Alsdann entfernt man die Körner, bestreut die Scheiben mit Zucker und läßt sie eine Zeitlang stehen Nun rührt man 4 Eier mit 8 Löffeln Mehl, 6 Löffel Weißwein, tunkt die Apfelscheiben in den angerührten Teig und läßt sie auf gelindem Feuer in Butter braun backen. Man servirt bestreut mit Zucker.

Louise Stein.

TAFFY. — 2 cups dark brown sugar, ½ cup butter, 4 tablespoons syrup, 2 teaspoons water, 2 teaspoons vinegar. Boil ½ hour, put into buttered tins to cool.

Eline Carr.

BUTTER SCOTCH CANDY. — ½ cup sugar, ½ cup molasses and ½ cup of butter. Boil until it will harden in water and then pour in a buttered tin and cut in squares.

Annie Petersen.

WHITE SUGAR CANDY. — 2 cups granulated sugar, 6 tablespoonfuls of water and 3 of vinegar. Let boil without stirring until it hardens when dropped in cold water. Let cool on buttered plates and pull till white and brittle. Flavor while pulling.

Miss Keim, Chillicothe, O.

POTATO PAN CAKES. — Grate potatoes in dish till you have one quart. Fill remainder of dish with water, then strain through cloth. Repeat this process, always using fresh water, until potatoes are white, when water should be thoroughly pressed out. The water used in washing potatoes should be allowed to settle, so as to obtain the starch. Have ready ½ pint boiling milk, pour over potatoes, stir and allow to cool. Now pour water off of starch and add to potatoes, also ¼ loaf baker's white bread soaked in milk, and lastly 3 thoroughly beaten egs. Salt to taste. If batter should be a little too stiff add more milk. Fry to a crisp brown in hot lard. Best eaten with apple sauce.

Mrs. J. Gross.

FRIED OYSTERS. — Drain thoroughly, season with pepper and salt, then dip one by one in powdered cracker, fry in butter, serve hot.

Mrs. M. Emmerich.

Gekochter Fisch. — 2 Pfund Fische, 2 Zwiebeln, 2 bis 3 Petersilien Wurzeln, stelle sie mit kaltem, scharfen Salzwasser auf ein rasches Feuer; schäume. Dann nimm 1 Löffel voll Butter und einen voll Mehl, rühre zusammen. Nachdem die Fische 3 Minuten gekocht haben, gieße die Brühe langsam auf die Butter, rühre, schütte zurück auf die Fische, gieb etwas grob gemahlenen Pfeffer dazu und laß 2 Min. kochen.

Frau Sraßheim.

Aal in Gelee. — Man setze in einem gut glasirten Kessel reichlich Wasser auf's Feuer, thue Gewürz, Lorbeerblätter, Zwiebeln, Petersilie, Salz und Essig hinzu und lasse es 5 Minuten kochen. Ist der Aal abgezogen oder abgerieben (je nach Belieben), ausgenommen, in Stücke geschnitten und gut gewaschen, so thut man ihn in das kochende Wasser und läßt ihn 15 bis 20 Minuten kochen. Dann nehme man ihn heraus, lege ihn in ein passendes Gefäß, lasse das Wasser noch einmal mit 5 bis 6 Blätter Gelatin und einem Eiweiß unter langsamen Rühren aufkochen und gieße es dann durch ein dichtes leinenes Tuch auf den Aal.

Anna Stein.

OYSTER PATTIES. ---- 2 oz. butter. ½ pt. sweet cream. 3 tablespoons flour, 3 doz. large oysters, pepper and salt to taste. Melt the butter, stir in the flour, boil the cream and stir in, cook oysters in their own liquor until cooked through, skim off liquor and add to the cream sauce. Fill the patties which are made of a rich puff paste.

Mrs. W. C. Webster.

BRAIN PATTIES. ---- Parboil a set or two of brains in water, then put them in cold water and pick off all dark skin. Take a frying pan, put in a spoonful of butter, a teaspoon of minced onion and a tablespoon of minced parsley; add the brains, 2 eggs, spoon of milk and scramble over fire like scrambled eggs. While cooking add a little nutmeg, juice of ½ lemon, pepper and salt. Bake puff paste patty cakes, take out lids, remove surplus paste from inside, fill with brains, put on lids, serve garnished with parsley.

Mrs. F. Fischbeck, Pasadena, Cal.

BOILED TROUT. — Clean fish thoroughly, put in boiling water with salt and 3 tablespoonfuls of vinegar. When fish is boiled enough, place on a large platter to dry. Then make a sauce of 1 quart of water, 1 pt. of green or canned peas, 1 large carrot boiled and chopped fine, 1 good tablespoon of butter, thicken with flour, add a little salt, and pour over fish before serving.

L. Reich.

SIMPLE DRESSING FOR TURKEY. — Soak some dry bread, drain it, put in it 2 eggs, some sage, butter size of an egg, season with salt and pepper, mix up good. Some prefer raisins in it, but it is good without.

Mrs. Lena Mohr.

OYSTER DRESSING. — To 1 quart of oysters take 1 lb. of oyster crackers, broken and moistened with hot water. Add 2 large tablespoonfuls of butter, 2 bunches of celery, chopped fine, pepper and salt to taste.

Mrs. G. Jacobs.

MACARONI. — Cook macaroni in water until soft, then put in a deep dish with alternate layers of grated crackers and cheese, a little salt, fill up the dish with milk and bake one hour.

Mrs. J. H. Haake.

BRETZELS. — 1 lb. flour, ½ lb. butter, ½ lb. sugar. Rub to a sand, mix in 2 eggs, form into bretzels, brush with whites of eggs, dip in coarse sugar. Bake in hot oven.

Lizette G. Sonnenschein.

CORN CR JOHNNY CAKE. —— ½ cup sugar, 1 large tablespoon butter, 2 eggs, 2 cupfuls of corn-meal, 1 cupful of wheat flour, 2 teaspoonfuls baking powder, 1¼ cups of milk.

Clara Fehn.

CREAM MUFFINS. - - One pint of milk, 1 pint of flour, 3 eggs, yolks and whites beaten separately, a little salt and 1 teaspoonful melted butter. Put in gem pans and bake 20 minutes.

Gretchen Jacobs.

Erdbeersaft. — Man nimmt Erdbeeren und Zucker zu glei=
chen Theilen, legt beides lagenweise in eine Schüssel und läßt es 2 – 3
Stunden stehen bis der Saft gezogen hat, thut dann alles in den zum
Kochen bestimmten Topf und läßt es heiß werden (nicht kochen). Dann
legt man ein weißes Tuch über ein Gefäß, gießt das ganze darauf, daß
der Saft durchfließt (aber nicht auspressen) und setzt den Saft nochmals
auf's Feuer, läßt ihn 5 Minuten kochen, schaumt gut ab und füllt ihn,
wenn erkaltet, in sauber gespülte, ganz trockene Flaschen, verkorkt mit
neuen Korken und versiegelt die Flaschen gut. Einige Eßlöffel voll die=
sen Saftes in ein Glas Wasser ist für Gesunde und Kranke ein erquick=
ender Trank. Die Beeren können kalt als Compott gegessen oder auch
zu Marmalade benutzt werden.

Frau Katharina Becker.

Junge Hühner. — Junge Hühner werden in Stücke zerlegt
mit etwas Salz und Pfeffer bestreut. Sodann nimmt man einen Topf
mit festem Deckel macht dann Butter gelbbraun, legt die Hühner hinein
und läßt sie auf beiden Seiten braun werden. Sodann gießt man nach
und nach etwas süßen Rahm darüber und läßt sie so etwa ¾ bis eine
Stunde schmoren. Zuletzt macht man die Sauce mit etwas Wasser und
ein wenig Mehl zurecht.

Frau J. Schulz.

BOSTON BROWN BREAD. —— 1 cup of corn-meal, 1 cup of rye
flour, 1 cup of wheat flour, 1 cup of molasses, 3 cups of milk, 2
teaspoons of baking powder, a little salt, and steam 3½ hours,
then bake ½ hour.

Mrs. D. C. F.

BISCUITS. —— One quart of flour, 2 teaspoonfuls of baking
powder, 1 teaspoonful of salt, 1 tablespoonful of sugar, 1 tablespoonful of butter and 1 pint of milk. Mix flour, baking powder,
salt and sugar, rub in the butter and add milk; roll thin, cut in
square pieces and roll. Bake from 15 to 20 minutes in a quick
oven.

Anna Keim, Chillicothe, O.

PEACH ICE-CREAM. ---- One quart cream, 1 pint of milk, 1 quart of peaches put through a sieve, 2 cups of sugar, whites of 2 eggs beaten to a stiff froth. Put the milk on to boil in a farina boiler. When hot, add the sugar and stir until dissolved. Take from the fire, add the cream, and when cold add the eggs and freeze. When half frozen add the peaches and finish until frozen enough. By letting it stand 2 to 3 hours packed, greatly improves it.

Mrs. J. Rearden.

BANANA ICE-CREAM. ---- ½ doz bananas, 2 eggs, 2 cups sugar, 1 quart milk, ½ quart of cream. Slice the bananas and put through a sieve; heat the milk to a boiling point; beat sugar and eggs together, add cream gradually, pour in the heated milk, while beating the other ingredients. While cool add the bananas and freeze.

Katherine Wissler, Chillicothe, O.

VANILLA ICE CREAM. ---- One quart of cream, 1 pint of milk, 2 cups of sugar, 1 large tablespoon of vanilla, whites of 2 eggs beaten to a stiff froth. Put the milk on to boil in a double boiler. When hot add the sugar and stir until dissolved. Take from the fire and add the cream, and when cold add the eggs and freeze. Pack it well until wanted.

Mrs. J. Rearden.

GRAHAM OR CORN BREAD. ---- 1 quart of either Graham or corn meal, softened with boiling water. When cool add 1 cup molasses, 1 tablespoon salt and 1 pint of light sponge of bread dough. Make into loaves into pans. When light bake, and when you eat it think of

Anna Thomas, Springfield, La.

BERLIN PANCAKE. ---- Roll out dough slightly sweetened and shortened, as if for plain doughnuts, cut in discs like biscuits, put a teaspoon currant jam or jelly on the center of one, lay another upon it, press the edges tightly together with the fingers and fry quickly in boiling lard. They will be perfect globes when done, a little smaller than an orange.

Mrs. F. Fischbeck, Pasadena, Cal.

—133—

Harte Seife. — Entleere den Inhalt einer Büchse von Lewis' Patent Powdered 98 pro. Lye, in einen Steinkrug oder in ein eisernes Gefäß, mit zwei und einem halben Pint reinen Wasser, rühre es um bis sich die Lauge auflößt und laß es dann stehen, bis die Temperatur der Mischung eine Höhe von nicht über 80 Grad erreicht. Schmelze 5½ Pfund reinen Fettes, Talg oder Schmalz, in einer Pfanne und halte dasselbe so lange über dem Feuer, bis es völlig flüssig ist; nachdem dies geschehen laß das Fett stehen, bis die Temperatur desselben 120 Grad erreicht. Dann gieße langsam die Laugenlösung in das Fett und rühre die Flüssigkeit so lange um, bis Fett und Lauge völlig vermischt sind, und bis die Mischung wie Honig herabfällt. Man rühre langsam, doch nicht zu lange, damit sich die Lauge nicht wieder separirt, von 5 bis 15 Minuten ist lang genug, je nach der Beschaffenheit des Fettes und des Wetters. Gieß dann die Mischung in eine Form, für welche eine hölzerne Kiste genügt und bedecke dieselbe mit einem Tuche oder einem Teppich, laß es an einen warmem Platze 1 bis 2 Tage stehen und dann nehme die Seife aus der Form und schneide dieselbe in beliebige Stücke.

Frau H. Tewes.

———

Inhalts = Verzeichniß.

Kochbuch.

Geschäftsführer.

—137—